# Death
## of a Christian
## Nation

# Death
### of a Christian Nation

GOD & COUNTRY
PRESS

# Deborah J. Dewart
## ATTORNEY AT LAW

# Death of a Christian Nation

ISBN 13: 978-0-89957023-5
ISBN 10: 0-89957-023-2
First Printing—May 2010

Scripture quotations taken from the New American Standard Bible (NASB)®, Copyright © 1960, 1962, 1963, 1968, 1971, 1972, 1973, 1975, 1977, 1995 by The Lockman Foundation. Used by permission." (www.Lockman.org)

Scripture quotations marked (ESV) are from The Holy Bible, English Standard Version® (ESV®), copyright © 2001 by Crossway, a publishing ministry of Good News Publishers. Used by permission. All rights reserved.

Scripture quotations marked (NIV) are taken from the Holy Bible, New International Version®, NIV®. Copyright © 1973, 1978, 1984 by Biblica, Inc.™ Used by permission of Zondervan. All rights reserved worldwide.

Cover designed by Daryle Beam at BrightBoy Design, Chattanooga, TN

Interior design and typesetting by Kristin Goble at PerfecType, Nashville, TN

Edited and proofread by Dan Penwell, Rich Cairnes, and Rick Steele

Printed in Canada
15 14 13 12 11 10 –T– 7 6 5 4 3 2 1

In loving memory of

author,
H. CLAY REAVIS, JR.

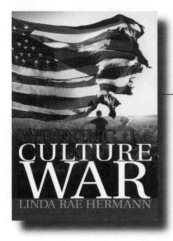
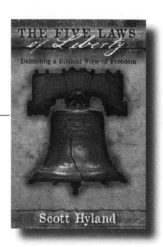

# Contents

# Acknowledgments

*Thanks* to beloved family members, and to my friends at Harvest Presbyterian (PCA) Church, who faithfully prayed and encouraged me in writing this book. Special thanks to Elder Tom Phillips, whose Wednesday night devotional message inspired the subsection, "Equal Protection Under the Cross," in Chapter 8.

Thanks to my law professor and co-counsel, James L. Hirsen, for providing the opportunity to write amicus briefs for the U. S. Supreme Court. The research for those briefs provided much of the background material for this book.

Thanks to my friends Mark and Kathy Lucas, founders of Community Discipleship Mission, who provided a bed, food, and computer—in a gorgeous mountain setting—during my final proofreading of the manuscript. My computer went down just when I needed to accomplish this final task!

# Foreword

To keep a civilization alive is no small task. A nation is born, often from turbulence, but always with promise of a better life for those persons who desire something better than what they experienced previously. But it is common that great nations of the past arose and fell within a few hundred years, the decay being so incremental that most of its citizens did not recognize the impending doom. The American experiment in liberty has gone down the same road. Those who came to the American shores sought for freedom under God. They wanted to escape persecution from those who wanted to dictate specific ways to think about and worship God. They wanted to be able to question political leaders without fear of punishment. In order to accomplish these goals they ventured out on an hazardous journey across the ocean and settled in places like Plymouth, Massachusetts and Jamestown, Virginia. But none of these travelers were attempting a government that had no religious foundation. They saw Christianity as the bulwark upon which to rest freedom. The recognition of the Supreme Deity was a necessary element in securing freedom for human beings, for without an absolute standard against which to measure human ideas and actions, there was no way to limit human despotism.

Freedom under God was the only way to assure freedom from statism in its various forms, whether it be the rule of a tyrannical king, rule by a class of elitists, or an overbearing president. By the time America was two hundred years old, the descendants of the Puritans and Pilgrims had established a government with limited powers. They accomplished this by dividing powers between states under a federal rather than a national government. Powers that were not specifically delegated to the federal government were reserved to the states or to the people. Obviously, these attempts to curb the insatiable appetites of politicians have been reversed over the last hundred years, with the people and states maintaining less power and a bloated federal government seeking national power over everything, albeit in the name of ministering to the general welfare of the people.

A truly free and democratic society must understand why it has become that way; freedom is no accident. A truly democratic system provides so much more than the ability to cast a vote, which some people believe to be the quintessential exercise of liberty. Sadam Hussein had voting in Iraq, even as President Mubarak has done in Egypt, with foregone conclusions, due either to government pressure or to the limited choice provided. The ballot has little value when those who vote have limited options for whom to vote, or they have little idea for what they are voting. The "liberty tree" in a constitutional republic includes the fruits of free speech, religion, and association, and that governmental leaders should derive their powers from the people. Yet these basic freedoms are being undercut in the United States. The general electorate has become uninformed about the nature of the proper limits of the federal government under our Constitution so that they don't even understand nor recognize the decay that is eating the foundation from under us.*

The tree of liberty has begun to rot at the roots, with license in the name of liberty, intolerance in the name of tolerance, rejection of *e pluribus unum* (out of many, one) in the name of diversity, repression of legitimate verbal disagreement in the name of "hate" speech, the exclusion of religion from the public square in the name

---

*"Many more Americans remember that Michael Jackson sang 'Beat It' than know that the Bill of Rights is part of the Constitution." (http://www.jeffersontoday. org/2009/12/04/83-percent-of-us-adults-fail-test-on-nations-founding/)

of separation of church and state. Our founders would not recognize the current tree from the one that they planted. Though our currency reads "In God We Trust"—a slogan found in the Supreme Court building and court rooms throughout the country—we trust little in the God worshipped by our founders, who gave us both life and liberty (Thomas Jefferson, *Summary of the Rights of British America*, July 1774).

There is considerable confusion in the minds of the people of the United States, and its leaders, in believing that rights may be given by the government for every desire and whim of the people. If a special interest group wants to do something contrary to the public good or public virtue as understood historically in human cultures or western jurisprudence (the basis of our law), ostensibly it has a right to do so and it should be protected by law. This civil right protection is not only to protect the behavior of a group, and as individuals, but prohibiting those who want to criticize such immoral behavior. This, however, may shut down political discourse within the public arena, as well as violate the ethical conscience of citizens. What happens in such cases is that guaranteed rights under the Bill of Rights of the U. S. Constitution lose their force in lieu of a supposed new right. Some of the misunderstanding comes from wrongly reading the Declaration where we are granted life, liberty, and the pursuit of happiness. What is usually not stated, however, is that these rights articulated by the Declaration are built upon the truth that we are under the laws of nature and the laws of nature's God and not civil rights merely given by the government. There is an objective and absolute standard. The equality that we are to experience under the law relates not to some superficial and forced equality contrary to nature but to the fact that God created us with rights. The Creator has given an inalienable right to life and yet abortion reigns in our land under a humanly created right of "privacy." The Creator has provided for liberty, and yet the government denies liberty of actions and conscience for persons who do not want to allow immoral acts in their own places of residence or business, or the lawful use of their personal and real property. Moreover, the Creator has given us the right to pursue happiness, but in the days of the Founders this referred to pursuing "blessedness" or bringing fulfillment to our lives in view of what God has given to us.

Progressives of today, unlike liberals of the eighteenth century, want to promote humanistic values contrary to the righteous virtues assumed, though not consistently practiced, in the founding of our nation, of moral responsibility and public virtue that reflected the Judeo-Christian worldview. Any civil or governmental rights were to be founded on human rights given by the Creator as stated in Declaration and articulated in the Constitution. The Declaration was in fact the theological foundation of the U. S. Constitution.

Deborah Dewart, in her book, *Death of a Christian Nation*, understands what I have said to this point. She recognizes that when civil law promotes immoral actions and anti-religious discrimination, the death of a nation is at hand. She correctly perceives that a righteous nation must be built on righteous laws and that in turn on the unchanging character of a righteous Creator. In the name of liberty and rights, America is becoming enslaved to puerile and ignoble "rights" that eat at the roots of the liberty tree and are a rejection of the principles that gave life to this great country. For a "mess of portage" we are selling our birthright as a people. I recommend her book as a *cure* for wrong thinking and correction to put us back on the right path envisioned by our Founders.

H. Wayne House, Th.D., J.D.

# Introduction

*My people are destroyed for lack of knowledge* (Hosea 4:6 ESV).

*A*merican Christianity is under attack. From shore to shore, cases are legion. Believers need knowledge. They need to know how fellow Christians are suffering for their faith right here in America. They need to know how current laws impact their ability to apply biblical principles in the workplace. They need to know their Bibles. They need to know where to turn for help. Without this knowledge, our "Christian" nation will die.

Some believers object to political action. After all, the church's mission is to preach the gospel, and we tread on dangerous ground when we perceive non-Christians as *the enemy* rather than persons who need Christ. We cannot idly stand by while fellow believers suffer serious legal consequences for practicing their faith. Moreover, our freedom to preach the gospel is rapidly diminishing, and preservation of that freedom is vital to the church and its mission. We must never forget our primary mission by becoming entangled in political warfare and neither can we hide our heads in the proverbial sand.

This text was inspired by my writing of an amicus brief[1] in a case decided by the California Supreme Court, where a homosexual woman sued two Christian medical doctors and a clinic for their refusal to perform a fertilization procedure enabling her to become pregnant with a child she planned to raise with her female partner. California has a broad sweeping civil rights law, the *Unruh Act*, that protects against all sorts of discrimination, including sexual orientation. This anti-discrimination law, covering every imaginable business establishment, is in some circumstances a frontal assault on the religious liberties of Christians who peacefully apply biblical principles in their businesses. Stiff legal penalties await a Christian contractor who refuses to build a temple for a cult or a Christian photographer who declines to take pictures for a same-sex wedding ceremony. A Christian lawyer could face a lawsuit and/or professional discipline for refusing to handle an adoption for a same-sex couple.

The lesbian plaintiff in California gave birth to a baby boy in 2001 after the Christian doctors referred her to another physician and even offered to pay her additional costs. Yet the case continued to wind its way through the courts until the final decision seven years later. Activists pursued the matter, setting dangerous precedent that threatens to crush the religious liberties on which America was founded. Under the guise of discrimination and access to public accommodations, homosexual activists attempt to force their opponents not only to tolerate but also to actively promote their morally objectionable agenda. This is a subtle form of slavery, compelling individuals to act against their deeply held religious convictions or face steep legal penalties. Such penalties include oppressive fines, professional displacement, or even shutting down a business. Battles rage on related fronts, as homosexuals demand the right to marry, adopt children together, divorce, and indoctrinate public school students. The homosexual agenda is setting the legal stage for persecution in our country unless we act wisely and swiftly to turn the tide.

But the homosexual agenda, dangerous as it is, is not the only threat. Christians are sometimes denied the right to speak on public streets about the moral issues of our day. Public schools muzzle our young children when they bring their faith into the classroom. College and graduate students risk their academic standing when they mix faith with "academic freedom." Nurses and pharmacists are demoted or even fired for refusing to participate in abortion or dispense the morning after pill. The public square erases religious expression as activists challenge prayer, nativity scenes, Ten Commandments displays, the Pledge of Allegiance, and even the simple inscription, *In God We Trust* on our coins. Newly minted civil rights, including sexual deviation and infanticide, dominate the American legal scene while religious wrongs are perpetrated on Christians who believe the First Amendment still protects their right to peacefully speak and practice their faith. There are multitudes of challenges, and we can only skim the surface in one book. However, skim it we must, because it's imperative that concerned Christians be equipped with both biblical and legal wisdom to face the challenges of our day.

*Part One*

# Sliding Down
# Slippery Slopes

# One

# Whatever Happened to "Christian" America?

*And if it is evil in your eyes to serve the Lord, choose this day whom you will serve . . . but as for me and my house, we will serve the Lord* (JOSHUA 24:15 ESV).

*Blessed is the nation whose God is the Lord* (PSALM 33:12 ESV).

On October 10, 2004, eleven Christians were arrested in Philadelphia for quoting the Bible at the annual Philly Pride homosexual "Outfest." Charges were ultimately dropped, and these believers sued the city officials who violated their free speech rights. Sadly, the Third Circuit Court of Appeals dismissed their case.[1]

*I*n the beginning, God blessed America. Christianity was the bedrock of this country. People found a safe refuge when they came to our shores to escape religious tyranny abroad. The right to freely worship God was guaranteed with the drafting of our Constitution and the Bill of Rights. The biblical principle of morality is the basis of our laws. America is not a theocracy like ancient Israel.

Early Americans chose to serve the Lord and establish a nation where citizens could freely worship God according to conscience and practice biblical principles without fear of state retribution. A nation whose God is the Lord.

Our founders repeatedly affirmed their reliance on the God of the Bible. Thomas Jefferson, who first penned the often-quoted phrase *separation of church and state*, cautioned against discarding our religious roots:

> And can the liberties of a nation be thought secure when we have removed their only firm basis—a conviction in the minds of the people that these liberties are the gift of God? That they are not to be violated but with His wrath? Indeed I tremble for my country when I reflect that God is just: that His justice cannot sleep forever.[2]

Benjamin Franklin, citing Scripture, issued a similar warning to early Americans: "If a sparrow cannot fall to the ground without His notice, is it probable that an empire can rise without His aid? We've been assured in the sacred writing that, 'Except the Lord build the house, they labor in vain that build it.'"[3]

John Adams, our second President, would be accused by today's liberals of violating the sacred wall of church-state separation when he said that: "We have no government armed with power capable of contending with human passions unbridled by morality and religion. . . . Our constitution was made only for a moral and religious people. It is wholly inadequate to the government of any other."[4]

For decades, courts at all levels presupposed that America was a Christian nation. An early Pennsylvania case resulted in a man's blasphemy conviction for speaking against Christianity and calling the Holy Scriptures a mere fable. The ACLU would have loved to litigate this one.

Christianity—all-inclusive Christianity—is, and always has been a part of the common law of Pennsylvania; This Christianity is without the spiritual artillery of European countries, for this Christianity was one of the considerations of the royal charter. The very basis of what William Penn founded was not Christianity based on any particular religious tenets, nor Christianity with an established church, and tithes, and spiritual courts; but, Christianity with liberty of conscience to all men.[5] A case that reached the U.S. Supreme Court in 1892 based its decision on America's Christian foundation after citing extensive evidence. A church was charged with violating a federal law that prohibited employers from hiring foreign laborers after the church contracted with a pastor from England. They were charged with violating a federal law that prohibited employers from hiring foreign laborers. The Court found the law inapplicable to the church because of the overwhelming evidence that America was a *Christian nation*, and therefore, Congress would never have intended to charge a church with a misdemeanor for hiring a foreign pastor:

> . . . no purpose of action against religion can be imputed to any legislation, state or national, because this is a religious people. This is historically true. From the discovery of this continent to the present hour, there is a single voice making this affirmation.[6]
>
> These [numerous state court cases, the Declaration of Independence, the Mayflower Compact of 1620, and other sources], and many other matters which might be noticed, add a volume of unofficial declarations to the mass of organic utterances that this is a Christian nation.[7]

Even into the twentieth century, courts continued to confirm the Christian character of this country:

> When he speaks of putting his allegiance to the will of God above his allegiance to the government, it is evident, in the light of his entire statement, that he means to make *his own interpretation* of the will of God the decisive test which shall conclude the government and stay its hand. We are a Christian people (Holy Trinity Church v. United States, 143 U.S. 457, 470–471), according to one another the equal right of religious freedom, and acknowledging with reverence the duty of obedience to the will of God. *But, also, we are a Nation with the duty to survive; a Nation whose Constitution contemplates war as well as peace; whose government must go forward upon the assumption, and safely can proceed upon no other, that*

> *unqualified allegiance to the Nation and submission and obedi-*
> *ence to the laws of the land, as well those made for war as those*
> *made for peace, are not inconsistent with the will of God.*[8]

This case that involved the naturalization of a Canadian, was later overruled as to the requirements for U.S. citizenship, but it stands as a testimony to the judicial affirmation that America is—or at least was—a Christian nation.

These early cases, affirming Christianity and its moral values, did not require non-Christians to engage in behavior contrary to their own consciences nor to actively endorse, practice, or otherwise facilitate the Christian religion. Citizens holding divergent religious viewpoints tolerated and lived at peace among one another. Times have radically changed, and now some aggressive non-Christians demand far more than peaceful coexistence. Under the guise of tolerance and diversity, Christians are being silenced in the expression of their faith and even compelled by law to actively facilitate political agendas repugnant to their deeply held religious convictions. If modern liberal activists have their way, the phrase *God Bless America* will ring hollow because our *Christian nation* will be dead. God will no longer bless a nation that has so thoroughly cast aside even the most basic tenets of His moral law.

# Two

# Lemon and Sherbert: Rebuilding the Wall of Separation

*First of all, then, I urge that supplications, prayers, intercessions, and thanksgivings be made for all people, for kings and all who are in high positions, that we may lead a peaceful and quiet life, godly and dignified in every way* (1 TIMOTHY 2:1–2 ESV).

When a Christian librarian in Kansas City, Missouri asked to have Sundays off because of her religious convictions, she was fired for insubordination. It took an action in federal district court to vindicate this Christian employee's rights under the Federal Civil Rights Act.[1] How could this happen in America—a nation under God founded on biblical principles with liberty and justice for all?

For decades, Americans enjoyed the right to worship God according to conscience without fear of government intrusion. They were free to lead quiet godly lives—to worship God and spread His gospel. The original church-state wall of separation protected religious belief and practice, but recent court decisions have created a different wall that protects unbelievers from unwelcome exposure to religious expression. This new freedom *from* religion is rapidly replacing our freedom *of* religion. *Of* and *from* may be small words, but the difference is huge, because freedom *from* religion implies the right to inhibit the religious liberty rights *of* other people. That is what is happening in many American courts today. In fact, atheist legal activists in Madison, Wisconsin, actually formed an organization called the *Freedom From Religion Foundation*. This group claims to be an educational organization formed "to promote the constitutional principle of separation of state and church, and to educate the public on matters relating to nontheism."[2] Similar organizations include the *American Civil Liberties Union*,[3] *Americans United for the Separation of Church and State*,[4] and *People for the American Way*.[5]

In order to understand the current legal climate, Christians need to trace the legal history, including the *Lemon* and *Sherbert* decisions along with other key decisions of the U.S. Supreme Court. The phrase—*wall of separation*—is found **nowhere** in the Constitution. This wearisome metaphor has generated mountains of confusion and litigation, leading Americans astray from the intent of those who drafted the First Amendment.

The two Religion Clauses of the First Amendment are contained in *one* phrase that seamlessly protects religious freedom:

> Congress shall make no law respecting an establishment of religion or prohibiting the free exercise thereof; or abridging the freedom of speech, or the press; or the right of the people peaceably to assemble, and to petition the government for a redress of grievances.

The Establishment Clause and the Free Exercise Clause are two complementary sides of the same coin: the first guards against improper state coercion and the second guards against unwarranted interference with religious exercise. They work together to guard religious freedom. The state may neither force a citizen *to* attend or support a church nor prevent a citizen *from* supporting or attending a church. Government may neither compel nor prohibit religious exercise.

## Thomas Jefferson's "Wall"

The term—wall of separation—was coined by then President Thomas Jefferson in a letter to the Danbury Baptists in 1801. The Baptists were gravely concerned about the preservation of religious liberty. They feared that the new constitution did not clearly acknowledge religious freedom as an inalienable, God-given right rather than a privilege granted by the state that could someday be regulated or removed. Here is what Jefferson said in response to their concerns:

> Believing with you that religion is a matter which lies solely between man and his God; that he owes account to none other for his faith or his worship; that the legislative powers of government reach actions only and not opinions, I contemplate with sovereign reverence that act of the whole American people which declared that their legislature should "make no law respecting an establishment of religion or prohibiting the free exercise thereof," *thus building a wall of separation between Church and State.*[6] (author's italics)

Jefferson recognized religious freedom as an inalienable, nonnegotiable right that must be zealously guarded. The intention of the term—*wall*—was to protect the inalienable right to worship God, free from state interference. Unlike modern courts that cite the *wall* only when deciding Establishment Clause cases, Jefferson's letter to the Baptists also encompasses the *Free Exercise Clause.* Today's wall of separation, protecting unbelievers *from* religion, is *not the wall* erected by the founders to protect the right of believers *to* worship. The original wall has been demolished and a **counterfeit** now stands in its place.

This reconstruction project began when Jefferson's wall of separation language was yanked away from its context. That first occurred in the *Reynolds* judgment, an 1878 decision rejecting the notion that religious liberty extended to the Mormon practice of polygamy. The Supreme Court cited Jefferson's wall of separation language and stated that: "Coming as this does from an acknowledged leader of the advocates of the measure [the First

Amendment], it may be accepted almost as an authoritative declaration of the scope and effect of the amendment thus secured."[7]

This one phrase extracted from Jefferson's personal letter to a particular group of his political supporters has resulted in years of jurisprudence being built upon it.

## The First Brick is Laid

A squabble over school bus money in 1947 hit the U.S. Supreme Court and began to revolutionize the way courts were to interpret the First Amendment.[8] The Court considered a New Jersey law that reimbursed parents as discriminatory, because funds for bus fare were being provided to send children to either a public or private accredited school. This providing of funds was viewed as a violation of religious freedom because certain families were *excluded* who chose to send their children to private religious schools. The court reached the reasonable, unremarkable conclusion that the state law was constitutional.

The *Everson* decision includes considerable history about religious freedom in America. Early settlers came to our shores from Europe to escape the tyranny of laws that forced them to attend and financially support government-controlled churches. However, charters granted by the English Crown authorized religious establishments in America that compelled believers and unbelievers alike to support and attend churches in the new colonies. The same pattern of persecution developed. People were thrown in jail, fined, tortured, and even killed as believers of different faiths began to torment one another and force compliance with government-run religion. Legal penalties were enforced for all sorts of religious offenses: failure to attend church, failure to pay taxes and tithes to support state-established churches, and even expressions of disagreement with religious doctrines. Protestant sects, Catholics, Quakers, Baptists, and Jews were all impacted. Those who belonged to a minority faith had to endure persecution for worshipping God according to conscience.

This had to stop. Early Americans soon realized that religious liberty was best achieved and maintained under a government stripped of the power to either coerce or interfere with religion.

The "Virginia Bill for Religious Liberty," originally written by Thomas Jefferson, says that, "Almighty God hath created the mind free. . . . [T]o compel a man to furnish contributions of money for the propagation of opinions which he disbelieves, is sinful and tyrannical."[9]

The *Everson* court reached a reasonable decision with considerable background about the true meaning and purpose of the Religion Clauses. But one short statement has been ripped out of context to justify a legion of litigation designed to erase our religious heritage and purge the public square of religious expression: "The *First Amendment* has erected a wall between church and state. That wall must be kept high and impregnable. We could not approve the slightest breach."[10]

## Construction Continues

Following *Everson*, a pair of cases considered programs that allowed public school students to spend part of their classroom time in religion classes. In the 1948 *McCollum* case, the Supreme Court ruled against a "released time" plan where Jewish, Catholic, and Protestant teachers entered public schools at specified times each week, during regular school hours, to teach their particular religion course. Participation was strictly voluntary, and students who chose not to attend remained in their classrooms to study secular subjects. The Court concluded that the Establishment Clause was being violated. Why? Because public funds were being used to spread religious faith on tax-supported property during compulsory school hours. Even so, the Court acknowledged that: "Devotion to the great principle of religious liberty should not lead us into a rigid interpretation of the constitutional guarantee that conflicts with the accepted habits of our people."[11]

Four years later, the Court considered a challenge to a New York law that allowed public school children, with parental permission, to attend religious classes *off campus* during school hours. This time, the Court upheld the program because there was no coercion and no religious instruction occurred on public property or at public expense. The Court explained that:

The First Amendment does not say that in every and all respects there shall be a separation of Church and State. . . . Otherwise the state and religion would be aliens to each other—hostile, suspicious, and even unfriendly.[12]

Although *Zorach* was a favorable decision for religious liberty, an ominous separation had begun. Religion was being slowly squeezed out of public schools and public life. School children could only be exposed to religious faith outside the doors of the classrooms, yet it was in these classrooms where they spent most of their waking hours during the week.

## A Firmer Foundation: Your Tax Dollars at Work

The Court can only decide a constitutional law case that is brought by a person who has standing to pursue it. "Standing" requires the plaintiff to have personally suffered an injury that will be remedied by a favorable court ruling. Mere disagreement is not enough.

But one important case in 1968 opened the floodgates to Establishment Clause litigation.[13] Seven taxpayers sued, alleging that the First Amendment was violated when federal funds were used to finance instruction and educational materials in religious schools. Their sole interest in the litigation was the manner in which their tax dollars were used. Many of us might object to the government's use of tax funds. Yet this 1968 case has multiplied the opportunities for activists to use their status as taxpayers to challenge every sort of government expenditure that might happen to benefit religious groups.

## *Lemon* and Its Sour Seeds: The Bricks Pile Up

Salary supplements in Rhode Island and educational services in Pennsylvania converged at the steps of the U.S. Supreme Court in 1971.[14] Rhode Island, being concerned about the quality of education in private schools, passed the Rhode Island 1969 Salary Supplement Act to authorize a 15% salary supplement to private school teachers for time spent teaching secular subjects. In 1968, Pennsylvania enacted the Nonpublic Elementary and Secondary Education Act, allowing the Superintendent of Public Instruction to reimburse private schools for expenses related to specific secular subjects, including textbooks, instructional materials, and teachers' salaries. When the Supreme Court considered both laws in the landmark *Lemon* decision, a three-prong test was created for Establishment Clause cases. First, the law must have "a secular purpose." Second, it must neither advance nor inhibit religion. Third, it must not foster "excessive entanglement" between the government and religion. The Court admitted that the Rhode Island and Pennsylvania laws had legitimate secular purposes and did not advance religion, but both failed the entanglement test. The Pennsylvania reimbursement program could not be used to pay for any courses with religious subject matter. In order to enforce that restriction, the state would have to monitor the materials to distinguish religious from secular content—thus becoming entangled in religious doctrine.

These three prongs are not easy to apply. Litigants and legislators must strain to find a *secular* purpose for the slightest contact between state and religion. The *wall* is at best an imperfect and imprecise metaphor, so courts occasionally overlook a remote, indirect, or incidental benefit to religion. In light of America's rich religious history, it's virtually impossible to avoid every potential benefit to religion without trampling religious liberty.

Activists have systematically utilized the *Lemon* test to sanitize public places under the guise of following constitutional commands (Chapter 10). Passive public displays don't coerce anyone into affirming any particular religious belief or supporting a church, but these are regularly attacked by persons who claim legal injuries from merely having to view them. Ten Commandments monuments, nativity scenes, and war memorials have all been the subject of repeated legal attacks.

*Lemon* has also been used extensively to excise religion from the public schools (Chapter 11). Courts have removed prayer, Bible reading, simple invocations at graduations and athletic events, and even an innocuous "moment of silence." Even the most nominal financial aid to private religious schools is so closely scrutinized that a hodge-podge of conflicting legal precedent has developed over the years.

Establishment Clause decisions have definitely soured under the *Lemon* test.

## Lemonade?

Occasionally, the Court either ignores *Lemon* or makes "*Lemonade.*" Sometimes this happens because the benefit to religion is the result of independent individual choices rather than government action. Applying *Lemon*, the Supreme Court ruled that a visually impaired student, attending Christian college to become a minister, was eligible for vocation rehabilitation assistance.[15] Similarly— but without applying *Lemon*—a deaf student attending Catholic school was entitled to a sign-language interpreter under the Individuals with Disabilities Education Act (IDEA).[16] IDEA created a neutral program with benefits to the students—not the schools they attended. Federally funded supplemental education, provided to disadvantaged students on a neutral basis, passes constitutional muster.[17] The Court also upheld a program that provided tuition aid to private school students and tutorial aid to public school students, based on the individual choices.[18]

Sometimes government funds may be made equally available to faith-based and secular organizations. The Court held in 1988 that religious organizations were eligible for federal funding under the Adolescent Family Life Act to provide services related to adolescent sexuality and pregnancy.[19]

The Court is sometimes more lenient when colleges or universities are involved, rather than elementary or secondary schools with impressionable young children. Federal construction grants to colleges and universities under the Higher Education Facilities Act were approved the same year *Lemon* was decided.[20] Several years later, the Court upheld a state subsidy program that allowed church-affiliated colleges to participate so long as the funds were segregated and not used for sectarian purposes.[21]

On occasion the Court acknowledges the vast religious heritage of America and ignores *Lemon* altogether. This happened in 1983 when state officials challenged the Nebraska legislature's long-standing practice of opening its sessions with a brief word of prayer.[22] When atheist Michael Newdow challenged the words "under God" in the Pledge of Allegiance recited at his daughter's school, the Supreme Court concluded that he could not bring the suit because he was not the custodial parent. But the concurring opinion of Justices Rehnquist, O'Connor, and Thomas includes extensive recognition of America's religious roots—supporting the Pledge.[23]

## One Small Victory

Court decisions cut both ways. The First Amendment is violated when the state exhibits callous indifference or hostility to religion. In May 2009, the United States District Court in Central California ruled in favor of a Christian high school student subjected to ridicule by a teacher who openly attacked his faith in class. The student cited twenty objectionable statements in his lawsuit. The Court held that the teacher violated the Constitution when he called creationism "superstitious nonsense."[24] Although the Court found that only this one statement actually violated the Establishment Clause, and the case is currently on appeal to the Ninth Circuit, this favorable decision is encouraging and worth celebrating.

## Let Freedom Ring

Although the First Amendment integrates the two Religion Clauses to protect religious liberty, judicial decisions have split them. The three *Lemon* factors have controlled many court rulings on the Establishment Clause, while other standards have developed independently for Free Exercise claims.

One early Free Exercise case involved mail fraud claims against organizers of the religious "I Am" movement, who made representations of supernatural healing powers in conjunction with solicitations for money.[25] The focus was on whether the Court could inquire into the actual truth of the Ballards' representations—or only the sincerity of their religious beliefs, regardless of actual truth. The Court concluded that it could only examine sincerity.

There was a time when religious oaths were required to hold public office. That all changed in 1961 when Roy Torcaso, an atheist, challenged the Maryland law that required him to affirm a belief in God in order to take the office of notary public.[26] That case upheld the view that the government could not treat *believers* and *unbelievers* differently. It also expanded the definition of religion to include nontheistic systems such as Buddhism, Taoism, ethical culture, and even secular humanism. A few years later, the Court struck down a Tennessee law that banned ministers from holding public office or serving as delegates to state constitutional conventions.[27] Citizens enjoy both the right to religious liberty and the right to seek public office. This law was enacted to ensure church-state separation, since clergy had exercised significant influence over political affairs in the past, but it was unconstitutional. Why? Because persons like Paul McDaniel, the ordained Baptist minister who filed suit, could not exercise both rights at the same time.

The most widely recognized set of Free Exercise criteria emerged in the 1963 *Sherbert* decision.[28] Adell Sherbert was a Seventh Day Adventist employed by a South Carolina textile mill. She was required to work on her Sabbath (Saturday) when the mill went from a five-day work week to a six-day work week. When she refused to comply, her employer discharged her. She applied for unemployment benefits but was disqualified because of her refusal to work on Saturdays. Her religious convictions were not deemed a "good cause" for her to be unavailable for Saturday employment. The Supreme Court found the disqualification unconstitutional, because it imposed a substantial burden on her religious freedom, penalizing her for the exercise of her constitutional liberty. A three-factor Free Exercise test developed from *Sherbert*. A successful Free Exercise challenge requires: (1) a sincerely held religious belief (as in the 1944 *Ballard* case above), (2) a substantial burden on that belief, and (3) lack of a compelling government interest that cannot be accomplished in a manner less restrictive of religious freedom. *Sherbert* acknowledged that conduct may be regulated, even where religiously motivated, if it poses a substantial threat to public safety, peace, or order. An employee's refusal to work on the Sabbath poses no such threat.

*Sherbert* has been applied and fine-tuned in several later cases. A Jehovah's Witness could not be denied unemployment benefits when he quit a job that required him to participate in the production of weapons.[29] Paula Hobbie, a Florida retail jewelry store employee who joined the Seventh-Day Adventist Church a couple of years *after* beginning her job, could not be denied unemployment benefits for "misconduct" related to her work.[30] Membership in an established church or religious sect is not required. A temporary retail worker who refused to work on Sundays could not be denied unemployment compensation merely because his beliefs were not based on the tenets of an established sect.[31]

The free exercise of religion does have limitations. Special exemptions from Social Security tax have been enacted to protect the religious convictions of ordained ministers generally and self-employed Amish persons in particular. But an Amish employer cannot opt out of paying the tax on employee wages, because the government has a compelling interest in maintaining the Social Security system.[32] Employers must attempt to accommodate employees' religious beliefs under the Civil Rights Act of 1964, but they're not required to do so if the accommodation would cause substantial hardship.[33] In military and prison settings, religious liberty still exists but officials have greater discretion in view of the special contexts.[34] Moreover, the Free Exercise Clause concerns what government cannot demand from the individual—not what the individual can demand from the state. The Supreme Court rejected a welfare applicant's objection to having a social security number assigned for his daughter in order to process welfare benefits and food stamps.[35] Similarly, but on a much larger scale, Native American Indians lost when they challenged a government decision to construct a paved road through federal land in the Six Rivers National Forest—land that they considered sacred and used for religious rituals that depended on silence and privacy.[36]

Free Exercise does not include the right to invade decisions about internal government procedures or the use of government-owned property.

For decades, the Free Exercise Clause protected religious liberty and generated minimal conflict, but that all changed in 1990 when the U.S. Supreme Court dropped a bombshell on the First Amendment.

*Three*

# Peace, Peyote, and Public Policy

*Let every person be subject to the governing authorities. For there is no authority except from God, and those that exist have been instituted by God* (ROMANS 13:1 ESV).

*But Peter and the apostles answered, "We must obey God rather than men"* (ACTS 5:29 ESV).

A lesbian in southern California sued two Christian medical doctors under the state's anti-discrimination law for refusing to perform a fertilization procedure that would enable her to become pregnant with a child she intended to raise with her female partner. The doctors claimed nothing more than the right to peacefully decline business where the services requested would conflict with their religious convictions. But in 2008 the California Supreme Court ruled against them.[1]

hen America's laws were grounded in biblical principles, obedience to civil law rarely threatened believers with a conflict between God's law and man's law. That is rapidly changing, and the problem is compounded by a controversial 1990 U.S. Supreme Court decision (*Smith*) involving two-drug rehab employees claiming a religious exemption from Oregon's criminal laws against peyote.[2] The Court held that government has no obligation to carve out religious exemptions from laws that are neutral and generally applicable. The application of this decision is disastrous where a believer seeks the right to peacefully "do nothing" in the face of a state mandate to sin.

## Peace or Penalty

Christians would not dispute the power of government to penalize evil conduct that disturbs peace and order. The Bible describes the civil authority as "an avenger who brings wrath on the one who practices evil" (Romans 13:4), ordained by God "for the punishment of evildoers" (1 Pet. 2:13–14). The law is made for the "lawless and rebellious . . . ungodly and sinners" who practice all sorts of wickedness—murder, kidnapping, perjury, sexual immorality, and the like (1 Tim. 1:8–11). Such lawless deeds, even if religiously motivated, are not protected under the rubric of religious liberty.

To understand the widely criticized *Smith* decision, we must first turn the clock back about a hundred years and examine the foundation for its reasoning. When America was still overwhelmingly governed by Christian principles, the Supreme Court heard two cases brought by Mormons. In the first one, George Reynolds challenged his conviction for bigamy because Mormon Church doctrine required its male members to practice polygamy. The Court quickly dismissed his Free Exercise argument. Civil government could rightfully intervene if religious practice broke out into "overt acts against peace and good order."[3] The Court explained that:

> Laws are made for the government of actions, and while they cannot interfere with mere religious belief and opinions, they may with practices. Suppose one believed that human sacrifices were a necessary part of religious worship, would it be seriously contended that the civil government under which

he lived could not interfere to prevent a sacrifice? Or if a wife religiously believed it was her duty to burn herself upon the funeral pile of her dead husband, would it be beyond the power of the civil government to prevent her carrying her belief into practice?[4]

The answers to these rhetorical questions followed naturally and generated little controversy at the time.

A few years later, another Mormon, Samuel Davis, was convicted for violating an Idaho statute because he falsely took an oath required for voters. The oath required him to state that he did not practice polygamy or belong to any organization—like the Mormon Church—that taught or encouraged it. Like Mr. Reynolds, he lost his religious freedom challenge in the Supreme Court that described polygamy as "a particularly pernicious crime that destroys society, disturbs families and degrades women."[5] The high court reasoned that the "free exercise of religion" is subordinate to the criminal laws of the country. If a sect advocated human sacrifice or sexual promiscuity, those acts would still be punished as criminal. Religious freedom was not a license for any sort of bizarre behavior but was integrally related to a biblical view of man's relationship and duties to the God of the Bible: "The term 'religion' has reference to one's views of his relations to his Creator, and to the obligations they impose of reverence for his being and character, and of obedience to his will."[6]

There was no uproar over the *Reynolds* and *Davis* decisions and no perceived threat to religious liberty. But one hundred years later, a legally similar decision would be catastrophic for Christians wanting to live their lives in obedience to the will of their Creator.

## Peyote or Pandemonium

The Book of Judges concludes with the ominous observation that "everyone did what was right in his own eyes" (Judges 21:25). The Supreme Court *(Smith)* decision in 1990 was driven by concerns that a similar pandemonium would break out if governments were required to carve out religious exemptions for every neutral, generally applicable law.

Alfred Smith and Galen Black, members of a Native American Church, were fired from their jobs with a private drug rehabilitation organization because they ingested peyote for sacramental purposes at a church ceremony. The Oregon Employment Division denied them unemployment benefits because they were terminated for work-related "misconduct."

Consumption of peyote was a criminal offense in Oregon, and state law offered no religious exemption. The Oregon Court of Appeals held that the denial of benefits violated their First Amendment rights, much like the Seventh Day Adventist in *Sherbert*, but the Oregon Supreme Court reversed that ruling. Unlike observing the Sabbath, ingestion of peyote was a criminal act. In a hotly contested decision, the U.S. Supreme Court agreed, distinguishing *Smith* from its earlier *Sherbert* decision:

> The *Sherbert* test is inapplicable to challenges to an across-the-board *criminal prohibition* on a particular form of conduct. The government's ability to enforce generally applicable prohibitions of *socially harmful conduct* cannot depend on measuring the effects of a governmental action on a religious objector's spiritual development. To make an individual's obligation to obey such a law contingent upon the law's coincidence with his religious beliefs, except where the state's interest is "compelling"—permitting him, by virtue of his beliefs, to become a law unto himself—contradicts both constitutional tradition and common sense.[7]

The *Smith* decision, written by Justice Scalia, held that religious beliefs do not excuse an individual from compliance with otherwise valid laws regulating conduct. An "otherwise valid law" means one that is *neutral* and *generally applicable*. The Court explained that the law prohibiting peyote consumption was not intended to restrict religious freedom. Therefore, it was neutral. *Smith* seemed consistent with many of the Court's earlier decisions, like *Reynolds* and *Davis*, where the Court upheld laws that criminalized polygamy over the objections of Mormons.[8] Child labor laws survived the challenge of a young Jehovah's Witness who accompanied her aunt to dispense religious literature in the evenings—believing she had a religious duty to perform such work.[9] Sunday closing laws trumped the rights of Jewish merchants whose religion required them also to close their businesses on Saturdays.[10] A self-employed Amish farmer could not opt out of paying Social Security tax on employee wages, in spite of his religious beliefs.[11] None of these neutral, generally applicable laws targeted religious practices, and some would have been justified in any event because they served compelling government interests.

Laws that *do* specifically target religious conduct violate the First Amendment unless they're necessary to achieve a compelling government interest. The Santeria Church in Hileah, Florida, composed largely of Cuban exiles, announced plans for a house of worship, school, cultural center, and museum. The community was alarmed because this sect practiced animal sacrifices in its religious rituals. The City Council reacted by hastily passing four ordinances that effectively outlawed the sacrifices. On the surface, the laws appeared to serve reasonable health and safety purposes. However, most animal killings other than the religious sacrifices were exempt. The fatal flaw was the law's intentional discrimination against the Santeria religious group. These ordinances were not neutral, so the Supreme Court struck them down.[12]

The *Smith* Court offered a limited "hybrid" exemption from its rule that religion does not excuse compliance with neutral, generally applicable laws. Where other constitutional rights accompany the Free Exercise claim—parental rights or free speech, for example—then the First Amendment may bar the application of an otherwise neutral law.[13] Parents have the right to send their children to private religious schools instead of public school,[14] and Amish parents may preserve their traditional religious way of life by electing not to send their teenage children to high school.[15] These are recognized exceptions to the neutral, generally applicable compulsory education laws. Similarly, free speech and religion claims combined in a case where the Court invalidated application of the compulsory flag salute to religious objectors.[16]

## Problems and Puzzles

Unlike earlier cases built on a comparable legal foundation, *Smith* dropped a bombshell on Free Exercise jurisprudence. *Smith's* reliance on those earlier cases—like *Reynolds*—must be considered in the context of America's religious roots. Shortly after *Reynolds*, the highest court in our land described America as a Christian nation. A moral foundation undergirds American law and public policies, and a century ago that foundation was substantially biblical. That is why, in 1879, the Supreme Court could uphold a so-called "neutral law of general applicability" without inciting the chaos generated by *Smith*.

The early American colonies were populated largely by Protestant Christians. America's founders, including Benjamin Franklin and Thomas Jefferson, spoke passionately about the religious underpinnings of our judicial system and cautioned against discarding our religious roots. Laws were compatible with religion and social mores. Government was less intrusive. Religion and law rarely conflicted, so there was little need to carve out exemptions. In those rare instances of conflict—oaths, military, religious assessments—religious exemptions were a familiar and accepted means of accommodation.

Protection for individual rights (liberalism) was originally linked to religion and supportive of religious freedom, but those connections have been severed. Liberalism now stands for "individualism, independence, and rationality." Freedom *from* religion has replaced freedom *of* religion in liberal thought.[17] *Smith* failed to consider that laws—deemed neutral in 1879—were derived from Christian doctrine. Modern liberal values risk the anarchy Justice Scalia feared in writing the *Smith* opinion because individual liberties have been ripped away from their religious heritage.

*Religious neutrality* is a myth. Laws regulating human conduct are based on someone's view of truth and morality. Religion is intimately concerned with truth and morality. Laws against polygamy are not religiously neutral. Neither are the laws that concern Christians today—abortion rights, laws that prohibit sexual orientation discrimination, and laws requiring evolution to be taught in public schools. It's these so-called neutral, generally applicable laws that often create a crisis of conscience for believers in their everyday lives when they operate businesses and go to work.

*Smith's* concerns about anarchy have little force in *conscientious objector* cases, which the opinion fails to distinguish from *civil disobedience* claims. Conscientious objectors don't become "a law unto themselves" when they obey the higher commands of God. The conscientious objector seeks to *passively* "do nothing," not to *actively* engage in socially harmful or criminal conduct. Religious Americans should not have to choose between allegiance to the state and faithfulness to God, particularly in situations where their beliefs can be easily accommodated without sacrificing public peace and safety. If morally shocking behavior—flag burning, computer-generated child pornography, profanity, cross burning—is protected as free expression, then surely Christians should be free to passively do nothing rather than be compelled to sin. Professionals should be able to decline business when asked to provide services that violate their deeply held religious convictions. Health care professionals and pharmacists should be able to opt out of participating in abortion-related services. Employees should not be disqualified from unemployment benefits on the basis of misconduct when rejecting a job that requires them to act against conscience. These situations don't correspond to the illegal drug use in *Smith* or the polygamy in *Reynolds*.

The Supreme Court has acknowledged that religious *exercise* is not limited to private beliefs unaccompanied by action. "[B]elief and action cannot be neatly confined in logic-tight compartments."[18] The First Amendment makes no distinction between religious belief and religious conduct, and there was no need to dissect them in earlier years of American history. There are a multitude of biblical commands to believers about conducting their lives in accordance with God's Word, to "walk in a manner worthy of the calling with which you have been called" (Ephesians 4:1). And while obedience to civil authority is a biblical principle, the call to obey God takes precedence in event of a conflict. As American law strays further and further from God's law, such conflicts rapidly multiply.

Besides these fundamental flaws, *Smith's* so-called "hybrid" exception defies logic. The Free Exercise Clause is rendered impotent and superfluous if it must be accompanied by an independent constitutional right. Nowhere does *Smith* explain why religious liberty, unlike other core rights, is too weak to survive by itself. This is troubling, because people originally came to our shores seeking the freedom to worship God according to conscience. Religious liberty is our *first* liberty, not a constitutional stepchild.

## Partners in Panic

Dissenting Justice Blackmun summarized the *Smith* decision as "a wholesale overturning of settled law concerning the Religion Clauses of our Constitution."[19] *Smith* has been widely denounced by courts, commentators, and other assorted critics. Panic over its implications had generated an unusual partnership among organizations and persons with diverse political and religious affiliations.[20] Criticism began within the opinion itself when Justice O'Connor concurred in the result, but severely criticized the Court's broad curtailment of religious freedom. O'Connor observed that *all* of our free exercise cases have concerned "generally applicable" laws that burdened religious practice. Even when laws serve compelling interests the Court can and should undertake a case-by-case analysis sensitive to the facts.[21]

In 1993, Congress enacted the Religious Freedom and Restoration Act (RFRA) in reaction to *Smith*, recognizing that even laws neutral toward religion can threaten religious freedom, and government should not substantially burden religious exercise without some compelling justification.[22] Congress announced its intent to restore the standards set forth in prior cases[23] and provide a defense to persons whose religious exercise is burdened by government.[24] In the same year RFRA was passed, Justice Souter urged the Court to reexamine *Smith* and proposed that a challenged law should be neutral in substance as well as form. The Free Exercise Clause protects against any unnecessary government interference with religion—not merely intentional discrimination.[25]

RFRA was a valiant effort to restore religious freedom, but it was only partially successful. In 1997, the Supreme Court decided an important case that would limit the scope of the Act to *federal* law.[26] St. Peter Catholic Church was situated on a hill in the City of Boerne, Texas, about twenty-eight miles northwest of San Antonio. This church, built in 1923, replicated the mission style of the region's earlier history. But it was growing rapidly and needed room to expand. Its 230-worshipper seating capacity was far too small. In order to meet the congregation's needs, the Archbishop of San Antonio gave the parish permission to enlarge the building. But the Boerne City Council passed an ordinance authorizing the city's Historic Landmark Commission to prepare a preservation plan with proposed historic landmarks and districts. The ordinance required the Commission's approval for construction affecting historic landmarks or buildings in a historic district. The Archbishop's application for a building permit was denied because St. Peter's was located in the historic district. The case ultimately reached the Supreme Court, which held that Congress exceeded its constitutional powers when it enacted RFRA. The Act was proper as applied to federal laws, but could not be applied to laws at the state or local level—like the city ordinance at issue. Congress had relied on the Enforcement Clause of the Fourteenth Amendment:

> The Congress shall have power to make all laws which shall be necessary and proper to secure to the citizens of each State all privileges and immunities of citizens in the several States, and to all persons in the several States equal protection in the rights of life, liberty, and property.

Congressional power under this clause is only remedial. There would need to be a widespread pattern of unconstitutional conduct requiring correction—perhaps a pattern or practice of state laws likely to be found unconstitutional—not merely one erroneous Supreme Court decision.

RFRA was applied in 2006 to facts reminiscent of *Smith*.[27] Members of a church with origins in the Amazon Rainforest receive communion by drinking hoasca, a hallucinogenic tea regulated under federal law. Church members successfully argued that they were entitled to a religious exemption. The government lost arguments about its compelling interests in the church members' health and safety, while trying to prevent the diversion of hoasca from the church to recreational users.

Congress acted again—this time in response to *City of Boerne*— by passing the Religious Land Use and Institutionalized Persons Act ("RLUIPA") in 2000.[28] This Act is more limited than RFRA, addressing only concerns about the use of land and religious accommodations for federal and state prisoners. The Supreme Court upheld this Act in 2005.[29] This recent case and RLUIPA are encouraging, but the battle for religious freedom in America is far from over. There is still much work to be done.

## Perilous Public Policies

Sometimes court decisions are grounded in public policy. No court will enforce a contract to murder for money. Public policies restrict contracts for surrogacy and adoption. The civil rights movement has created strong public policies in favor of racial integration and equal opportunities. Some of these well-established policies pose no danger to believers. But America's public policies are in a state of chaos and sometimes clash with values Christians hold dear. As new policies develop, Christians are increasingly at risk and may have to pay a high legal price in order to follow God's Word.

As Jesus prepared to ascend to heaven after His resurrection, He left instructions to go into *all* nations and make disciples (Matt. 28:18–20). Few believers today would condone racial or ethnic discrimination. But two Christian schools lost their tax-exempt status with the IRS because their unusual interpretation of Scripture supported racially discriminatory school policies.[30] Bob Jones University, located in Greenville, South Carolina, was formed as an educational and religious organization to teach and propagate fundamentalist Christian beliefs. Students were screened about their beliefs and the university expected them to abide by strict standards of public and private conduct. The school's sponsors believed the Bible forbids interracial dating. From 1971 to 1975, the university accepted applications from African-Americans who were married within their race—but not from those who were single. Goldsboro Christian Schools in North Carolina maintained a racially discriminatory policy, also based on its interpretation of Scripture. School officials believed race is determined by descent from one of Noah's three sons (Ham, Shem, and Japheth), and that cultural or biological mixing of the races is forbidden.

In order to qualify for tax exemption under IRS regulations, an educational organization must maintain a racially non-discriminatory policy. Bob Jones University and Goldsboro Christian Schools both lost their exemptions because of their religiously motivated discrimination. The Supreme Court upheld the revocations of exempt status because of the strong, overriding governmental interest in eradicating racial discrimination in education. The Court explained that the schools could still observe their religious doctrine—it would simply be more expensive to do so without the benefit of tax exemption.

The *Bob Jones* decision was driven by a strong public policy favoring the elimination of racial discrimination. Most Christians would applaud that particular policy in light of Scripture. But there is an emerging, public policy that advocates eliminating sexual orientation discrimination. The two types of discrimination are hardly analogous—race is based on a morally neutral trait, while sexual orientation is defined by conduct—but liberal courts are failing to acknowledge that critical distinction. When the California Supreme Court ruled against the Christian medical doctors in 2008, the Court relied heavily on *Smith* and found a compelling interest in eliminating sexual orientation discrimination:

> The [Unruh] Act furthers California's compelling interest in ensuring full and equal access to medical treatment irrespective of sexual orientation, and there are no less restrictive means for the state to achieve that goal.[31]

Although worded in terms of access to *medical* treatment—which no conscientious Christian physician would deny to anyone truly in need—the case was about an elective procedure for artificial insemination, not treatment for injury or disease. This case has ominous implications for Christians.

## Pathway to Persecution

By deferring to any apparently neutral law, the *Smith* decision jeopardizes the quality of religious freedom and sets the legal stage for religious persecution.[32] Concerns about federalism prompted the U.S. Supreme Court to reject the national attempt to preserve religious freedom in the aftermath of *Smith*, and that Court's failure to clarify or reevaluate *Smith* has resulted in a fragmented, state-by-state approach.[33] This is unfortunate, because it means that protection of a core constitutional right is left to the vicissitudes of the political process—exactly what the Constitution was intended to prevent. Nevertheless, state courts and legislators need to protect Americans from the harm that will result if a low threshold is set for applying laws that threaten their faith—including laws protecting abortion, broad-sweeping anti-discrimination laws that encompass sexual orientation, and laws recognizing same-sex marriage.

*Four*

# Appalling
# Applications

*Now he [Pilate] was obliged to release to them [the Jews] at the feast one man. But they all cried out together, saying "Away with this man [Jesus], and release for us Barabbas!"* (LUKE 23:17–18 NASB).

City officials used a noise ordinance to admonish and arrest Christian evangelists who had been sharing the gospel in the city's parks since 1978.[1] Staff members of American Christian Enterprises had received many permits from the City over the years for sound amplification to conduct their outreach activities, but in 1995 local police began responding to complaints from people who were hostile to their Christian message. Permits were denied and the evangelists were cited for disturbing the peace.

Meanwhile, other events continued undisturbed in spite of excessive noise levels: Cinco de Mayo Celebration (May 1996); the Making Waves musical heritage festival (June 1996); and the Gay Pride Celebration (June 1996).

*P*ilate was legally obligated to release one prisoner to the Jews at their feast. Rather than release the one truly innocent Man, the crowd demanded that Pilate release a murderer.

God used this travesty of human justice to accomplish our salvation (Acts 2:22–24), but the incident shows the appalling manner in which a law can be applied.

Christians are not being burned at the stake, but alarming applications of *Smith* and other seemingly innocuous laws have already imposed substantial legal penalties on believers who dare to practice their faith in daily life. A statute may appear neutral on its face, but in a particular situation, it may be unconstitutional as applied because it substantially burdens religion. Free speech and other expression is subject to reasonable restrictions on time, place, and manner. Christians can preach the gospel on the streets, but not necessarily using a bullhorn at 3:00 a.m. However, noise ordinances and discretionary permit laws can be wrongfully applied by hostile officials to squelch religious speech.

The same is true of other laws—particularly the escalating number of allegedly neutral, anti-disciminatory statutes that protect groups of people based on sexually immoral lifestyles. Such laws are particularly vulnerable to applications that decimate religious liberty. Christian doctors should not deny emergency care or a host of other necessary treatments on the basis of sexual orientation, but religion is substantially burdened where an anti-discrimination law requires a physician to act against religious conscience by fertilizing a lesbian who will raise her child in a "two-mother" home. A Christian property owner should ordinarily not discriminate against single tenants, but if forced to rent to an unmarried boyfriend-girlfriend or a homosexual couple, the law coerces that property owner to violate conscience by facilitating sin. All sorts of appalling applications are emerging in both federal and state courts. Even some ultimately favorable decisions are costly in terms of the time, effort, and expense involved in getting to a higher court.

### Room *Not* For Rent

*Smith v. Fair Employment and Housing Commission* (1996) 12 Cal. 4th 1143

Evelyn Smith, a widow, owned and leased two duplexes (four rental units) in Chico, California. She was actively involved in daily maintenance and depended on the rental income. But her livelihood came to an untimely end after she refused to rent to an unmarried boyfriend-girlfriend because of her religious conviction that God would judge her if she faciliated a sexual relationship outside of marriage. The California Fair Employment and Housing Act forbids discrimination in rental housing, based on a variety of personal characteristics—including marital status. This law could be rightly applied to ensure that single persons and married couples are all able to find affordable housing. Instead, the California Supreme Court found an implied right to fornication, callously ignoring the landlord's religious convictions and the financial hardship imposed on her if she could not rent her property.

Mrs. Smith objected to the sinful conduct of her potential tenants, not the fact that they were both single individuals. However, the state court concluded that she was discriminating on the basis of marital *status* rather than *conduct*, quoting from a similar case in Alaska:

> [A landlord] cannot reasonably claim that he does not rent or show property to cohabiting couples based on their conduct (living together outside of marriage) and not their marital status when their marital status (unmarried) is what makes their conduct immoral in his opinion.[2]

This sort of distorted rationale pervades the opinion, which relies heavily on the neutral-generally-applicable law from the U.S. Supreme Court *Smith* decision:

> The law is generally applicable in that it prohibits all discrimination without reference to motivation. The law is neutral in that its object is to prohibit discrimination irrespective of reason—not because it's undertaken for religious reasons.[3]

But when the law is applied so as to trample religiously motivated discrimination, it's hardly neutral. It's a blunt instrument applied to the First Amendment.

Incredibly, the California Supreme Court ruled that there was no substantial burden on Mrs. Smith's free exercise of religion. The justices reasoned that her religious beliefs did not require her to rent apartments, and she could avoid the crisis of conscience by simply selling her property and investing her capital elsewhere. Earlier cases have held that the Free Exercise Clause is not necessarily violated merely because a law operates to make the practice of religion more expensive.[4] Perhaps some economic costs are not unreasonable to bear, but this court's decision forced Mrs. Smith to either violate her conscience or abandon her business altogether—surely a substantial burden.

This court also focused on the allegedly "serious impact on the rights and interests of third parties"—the unmarried couple. The court noted their right to access public accommodations and "*the dignity interests in freedom from discrimination based on personal characteristics*."[5] Christians would not dispute consideration of the legitimate rights and interests of others. Love of God and neighbor is central to keeping God's commandments. But modern laws increasingly protect groups defined by their sexually immoral lifestyle (homosexuality) or their choices to engage in conduct the Bible defines as sin (abortion, fornication). The "right to sin" thus collides with the rights of believers to conduct their lives and businesses in accordance with Scripture.

## Don't Reign Over Our Parade

*Hurley v. Irish-American Gay, Lesbian, & Bisexual Group of Boston (1995) 515 U.S. 557*

The U.S. Supreme Court has ruled that anti-discrimination laws should not be applied so as to demolish First Amendment liberties. The *Hurley* court noted the expanding reach of such laws and held that the particular application of Massachusetts' statute infringed the parade organizers' rights, affirming our nation's commitment to protect expression regardless of content.

The South Boston Allied War Veterans' Council, an unincorporated association of private individuals, organized an annual St. Patrick's Day parade in Boston. The Council approved parade participants in confirmity with the message it chose to convey. In 1992, activists formed an organization (GLIB) of gay, lesbian, and bisexual Irish descendants in order to march in the parade and celebrate their lifestyle. The Council denied their application to participate, and they sued. *State courts ruled in their favor, concluding that the parade organizers had violated Massachusetts' anti-discrimination law.*

The U.S. Supreme Court receives many petitions for review but hears only a small percentage of them. The Court did not have to hear the parade council's case, but it granted their petition and rendered a favorable decision. The ruling was based on the rights to free speech and expression protected by the First Amendment. The parade was a form of expression, and a speaker has autonomy to choose the content of the message. The parade organizers could not be compelled to affirm belief in the message that GLIB wanted to promote. GLIB could organize its own independent parade and apply for a permit, but could not impose itself and its message on the St. Patrick's Day parade organizers.

The Court included some explanation about the history of anti-discrimination laws. At common law, innkeepers and others who operated places of public accommodation could not refuse to serve a customer without good reason. This simple, commonsense principle has been vastly expanded to encompass more places and more defined groups of protected people. The U.S. Supreme Court rightly recognized the potential First Amendment dangers in applying modern anti-discrimination laws to expressive activity, such as this parade. The *Hurley* case is good legal precedent for believers to cite when anti-discrimination laws threaten the expression of religious convictions.

## Boy Scouts: Honor and Dishonor

*Boy Scouts v. Dale* (2000) 530 U.S. 640; *Boy Scouts of Am. v. Wyman* (2d Cir. 2003) 335 F.3d 80

The Boy Scouts' commitment to youth and morality has landed it in the legal system more than once. Courts have both honored and dishonored the Scout Oath and Law, with its commitment to help youth become morally straight and clean.

James Dale was a former Eagle Scout who became assistant scoutmaster of a New Jersey troop. The Boy Scouts revoked his membership upon learning that he was an outspoken homosexual and gay rights activist. The organization did not want to promote homosexuality as a legitimate behavior or lifestyle. The New Jersey Supreme Court ruled that the state's public accommodations law required the Scouts to admit Dale.

Again, the U.S. Supreme Court was not obligated to hear the Boy Scouts' appeal, but it did. As in *Hurley*, the Court found that the particular application of state law violated the Scouts' First Amendment rights. The decision noted the expansion of public accommodations laws, beyond restaurants, shops, and libraries to more private places, like summer camps and even private membership associations not tied to a physical location.[6] As the reach of such laws expands, so does the potential for conflict with First Amendment rights. This time, the right at issue was freedom of association. The Court explained that "an association that seeks to transmit a system of values engages in expressive activity."[7] Such an organization cannot be forced to include members it does not want, if inclusion would jeopardize the group's ability to express its chosen message.[8] However, the Court also cautioned that: "An expressive association cannot erect a shield against antidiscrimination laws simply by asserting that mere acceptance of a member from a particular group would impair its message."[9]

In light of this warning, it's important for churches and other Christian groups to think carefully about how acceptance of a particular type of member would jeopardize its message. Besides the legal analysis, it's equally important to engage in clear biblical thinking in view of commands to reach the lost with the gospel—to live *in* the world but not be *of* the world. Jesus ate with sinners and offered them forgiveness, but He did not compromise His holiness.

Not all courts have honored either *Dale* or the Boy Scouts. Three years after *Dale*, the federal Court of Appeals for the Second Circuit upheld a decision of the Connecticut State Employee Campaign Committee that denied the local Boy Scouts' application to participate in the state's workplace charitable contribution campaign. This Appellate Court found the Boy Scouts' policy of excluding homosexuals to be in violation of Connecticut's Gay Rights Law. That law, the court explained:

. . . prohibits discriminatory membership and employment policies not because of the viewpoints such policies express, but because of the immediate harms—like denial of concrete economic and social benefits—such discrimination causes homosexuals.[10]

## School Days—Rule Days

*Christian Legal Society v. Walker* (7th Cir. 2006) 453 F.3d 853; *Christian Legal Society v. Kane* (N.D. Cal. 2006) 2006 U.S. Dist. LEXIS 27347

The Christian Legal Society (CLS) faced a pair of federal court challenges in 2006, both involving student chapters on campuses of public law schools. The facts are similar, but reasoning and results are about as far apart as east and west.

The dean of Southern Illinois University School of Law revoked the official student organization status of the student CLS chapter on campus because its membership policies excluded homosexuals (*Walker*). The student CLS chapter at the University of California, Hastings School of Law, met a similar fate when submitting its bylaws and application for travel funds to attend a national CLS conference (*Kane*). Both decisions arose out of a conflict between CLS requirements for voting members and officers, and the school's antidiscrimination policy. The student chapters welcomed everyone at their meetings—without discrimination—but voting members and officers were required to subscribe to a statement of faith and live by biblical standards. Practicing homosexuals were ineligible because the Bible condemns homosexuality as sin.

Official recognition for student organizations provides many benefits, including e-mail databases for communications, use of school facilities, posting on school bulletin boards, and funding for activities. Organizations can still exist without these benefits, but communication with the student body is far more difficult and activities must be funded without any help from the law school.

Christian students were victorious in the Seventh Circuit *Walker* case. This court noted that CLS is a faith-based, expressive organization that conveys messages about morality and sexuality. Forcing it to accept homosexuals and unbelievers "would cause the group as it currently identifies itself to cease to exist."[11] The court explained the unconstitutionality of the school's application of its policy:

> Antidiscrimination regulations may not be applied to expressive conduct with the purpose of either suppressing or promoting a particular viewpoint. While the law is free to promote all sorts of conduct in place of harmful behavior, it is not free to interfere with speech for no better reason than promoting an approved message or discouraging a disfavored one, however enlightened either purpose may strike the government.[12]

Other religiously defined groups—the Muslim Students Association and the Adventist Campus Ministries—had not been denied official recognition. The *Walker* court found that withholding the benefits of recognition from CLS was an impermissible interference with the student group's freedom to associate.

The *Kane* court analysis veered off in the opposition direction.[13] Even the court's description of the case—Factual Background—has a menacing tone:

> This case concerns whether a religious student organization may compel a public university law school to fund its activities and to allow the group to use the school's name and facilities even though the organization admittedly discriminates in the selection of its members and officers on the basis of religion and sexual orientation.

Hastings was committed to "a policy against legally impermissible, arbitrary, or unreasonable discriminatory practices," including discrimination based on sexual orientation. The court found this policy neutral and generally applicable, per *Smith*, and equated sincere religious conviction with *arbitrary* and *unreasonable* discrimination, thus making the judgment that biblical views of homosexuality are *arbitrary* and *unreasonable*. The court sidestepped the First Amendment by finding that the school policy regulated conduct— what CLS must *do* to become a registered student organization— rather than expression—what CLS may *say* about its Christian beliefs. The ruling against the students was premised on the principle that:

> Where the government does not target conduct on the basis of its expressive content, acts are not shielded from regulation merely because they express a discriminatory idea or philosophy.[14]

But it's difficult to believe that the law school did not target *conduct*—the student organization's religious requirements for members and officers—on the basis of its expressive *content*—namely, the biblical view of homosexuality that clashes with the school's antidiscrimination edict. In fact, the court proclaimed that states have a substantial and compelling interest in prohibiting discrimination based on religion and sexual orientation.

There are several cases *Kane* cites and attempts to distinguish from the CLS situation. These are all cases where courts overruled decisions of colleges or universities that refused to recognize a student organization. Nevertheless, they're cases where homosexual groups were the *target* of discrimination rather than the *beneficiary* of a non-discrimination policy:

- *Gay and Lesbian Students Ass'n v. Gohn* (8th Cir. 1988) 850 F.2d 361: The university refused to fund two films and a panel discussion because "we cannot use state money to support a homosexual group."
- *Gay Alliance of Students v. Matthews* (4th Cir. 1976) 544 F.2d 162: The university refused to recognize a homosexual student group because officials feared it would increase the opportunity for homosexual contacts and harm students affiliated with a homosexual activist organization.
- *Gay Students Org. of University of New Hampshire v. Bonner* (1st Cir. 1974) 509 F.2d 652: The university prohibited a homosexual student group from sponsoring social functions due to concerns about the distribution of extremist homosexual publications at such events.

Incredibly, the federal court in Northern California reached the conclusion that CLS had not demonstrated how admitting homosexuals or non-Christians would impair its mission. The mission of the student chapter was "to maintain a vibrant Christian Law Fellowship on the School's campus which enables its members, individually and as a group, to love the Lord with their whole beings—hearts, souls, and minds—and to love their neighbors as themselves."[15] Although we all continue to sin during this lifetime, loving the Lord involves keeping His commandments (John 15:10)—not exalting a lifestyle that normalizes what God has called sin. Placing unrepentant homosexuals in leadership positions or even admitting them to membership would rot the core values of the organization and ultimately destroy it.

## Gender Bender

*EEOC v. Fremont Christian School* (9th Cir. 1986) 781 F.2d 1362

The Book of Genesis teaches that both male and female are created in the image of God. While theological debates surround portions of Scripture concerning the differing roles of men and women,[16] many sincere believers are committed to maintaining the distinctions set forth in the Bible.

Freemont Christian School was a private institution, operated by the Assembly of God Church, serving children in preschool through twelfth grade. The school limited its health insurance plan to "head of household" employees—married men and single women—based on their understanding of Scripture that the husband is the head of the home and required to provide for it. In earlier years, the school paid male employees at a higher rate than female employees performing similar duties, but it abandoned that policy because of its illegality.

Ruth Frost, a married female employee, filed a complaint with the Equal Employment Opportunity Commission (EEOC) in 1981, based on Title VII of the Civil Rights Act of 1964. The Ninth Circuit Court of Appeals found that there was a compelling state interest in eliminating gender discrimination—compelling enough to override the sincere religious beliefs of the school.

## Compelling Contraceptives
*Catholic Charities of Sacramento, Inc. v. Superior Court* (2004) 32 Cal.4th 527

Another gender-related case was litigated in California against a nonprofit charity associated with the Roman Catholic Church. Catholic Charities was engaged in a variety of services, including counseling, immigration assistance, and low-income housing for the poor. The organization employed and served people of many faiths and backgrounds. However, its health insurance program excluded coverage for contraceptives because of the religious position of the Catholic Church. That collided with the Woman's Contraception Equity Act (WCEA) that neutrally and generally required all employers—regardless of religious affiliation—to include contraceptives if it offered insurance that included prescription drug coverage. An extremely narrow statutory exemption offered relief to a tiny number of religious organizations.

As with many other appalling applications, this one relies heavily on *Smith*, claiming that neutrality must rest on whether the object of a law is to suppress religion or religiously motivate conduct. Similarly, the California Supreme Court would find a law generally applicable unless it selectively imposed burdens *only* on conduct motivated by religious convictions.[17] Here, WCEA applied to all employers engaged in charitable work and did not expressly target those engaged in it for religious purposes, so it was deemed to pass the neutral-generally applicable test. In addition, the court concluded that WCEA served the state's compelling interest in eliminating gender discrimination.[18] Nonetheless, as the dissenting opinion observes, this case involves fundamental issues of morality that cannot possibly be labeled neutral:

> In the present controversy, one side posits that sex is an aspect of autonomy, a vital human function in which men and women should be able to engage, enjoying their sexuality "free from anxiety." (Hayden, *Gender Discrimination Within the Reproductive Health Care System: Viagra v. Birth Control* (1999) 13 J.L. & Health 171, 181.) This may in fact be the view of a majority of American adults. The Catholic Church's

view, in contrast, deems all forms of nonmarital sex immoral, and views sex within marriage as a unitive, procreative, and sacred reflection of a spiritual, emotional, and biological reality that comes complete with reproductive anxiety. (See George & Bradley, *Marriage and the Liberal Imagination* (1995) 84 Geo. L.J. 302–320.) This is a perspective many people would disparage as archaic. Several of the legislators debating the WCEA seemed to think so.[19]

The court also focused on how a religious exemption might detrimentally impact the rights of third parties—a recurring theme in cases where religious liberty conflicts with newly minted non-discrimination rights created by statute. This court would readily drive Christians out of the marketplace:

> Congress and the courts have been sensitive to the needs flowing from the Free Exercise Clause, but every person cannot be shielded from all the burdens incident to exercising every aspect of the right to practice religious beliefs. When followers of a particular sect enter into commercial activity as a matter of choice, the limits they accept on their own conduct as a matter of conscience and faith are not to be superimposed on the statutory schemes which are binding on others in that activity.[20]

But those statutory schemes increasingly impose the obligation to accept and even facilitate all sorts of sinful conduct. Nothing about that trend is "sensitive to the needs flowing from the Free Exercise Clause."

## All or Nothing

*Catholic Charities* and other cases like it not only force conscientious believers out of the marketplace but may ultimately be counter-productive. WCEA was intended to increase access to health care services for women, but Catholic Charities could only adhere to its religious convictions by discontinuing *all* prescription drug coverage for *all* employees. The provisions in *Fremont Christian School* were intended to ensure equal health insurance coverage for male and female employees, but again, the school could only hold to its view of Scripture by discontinuing coverage for *all* of its employees. Elimination of drug and medical insurances would harm *all* employees, including the *Catholic Charities* women who desired contraceptives and the female employees of Fremont Christian School. The Unruh Act at issue in *North Coast Women's* was supposed to increase access to public goods and services on a non-discriminatory basis, but the doctor defendants could only avoid violating their convictions by discontinuing fertility services for *all* patients. The provisions challenged in *Smith* (California) were designed to ensure broad access to housing, but the Christian property owner could only avoid violating her conscience by abandoning the rental of her property. Applying the law in a manner that stifles religious freedom may ultimately defeat its purposes and generate unnecessary harm to third parties, including customers and employees. Accommodation of religious freedom would ensure maximum availability of public goods and services.

## Alarming Applications

These are just a handful of the cases where neutral laws have been applied—or misapplied—to crush religious freedom in America. There are some good decisions, like *Hurley* and *Dale*, and others that defy law, logic, and respect for religious liberty. An increasing number of courts are applying so-called neutral laws in a manner that is anything but religiously neutral. Moreover, a law that reflects only one side of a morally controversial issue—like nonmarital sex—is hardly neutral.

*Five*

# Death, Liberty, and
# The Pursuit of Happiness

*Rescue those who are being taken away to death; hold back those who are stumbling to the slaughter. If you say, "Behold, we did not know this," does not He who weighs the heart perceive it? Does not He who keeps watch over your soul know it, and will He not repay man according to his work?* (PROVERBS 24:11–12 ESV).

It's legally risky to even speak against the seemingly sacred right to terminate an unborn child's life. Pro-life high school students in Virginia, New York, and Pennsylvania[1] needed an injunction from a federal judge in order to tell classmates why they oppose the Supreme Court's *Roe v. Wade* decision. Judicial intervention was necessary even though these students used purely peaceful means to communicate (leaflets and t-shirts) during the "Pro-Life Day of Silent Solidarity" in January 2007, a national student-led event sponsored by Stand True.

*"The first thing I'd do as president is sign the Freedom of Choice Act. That's the first thing that I'd do."—Senator Barack Obama, speaking to the Planned Parenthood Action Fund, July 17, 2007.*

*T*he "Freedom of Choice Act" was introduced in both houses of U.S. Congress "to protect, consistent with *Roe v. Wade*, a woman's freedom to choose to bear a child or terminate a pregnancy, and for other purposes."[2] This deadly legislation seeks to nullify any federal or state law that interferes with access to abortion.[3] It's especially troubling in light of the favorable Supreme Court decision upholding the Partial Birth Abortion Act of 2003.[4] The U.S. Constitution guarantees the right to *life* unless that right is taken through due process of law. The Declaration of Independence—America's birth certificate—acknowledges that persons are endowed by their Creator with certain inalienable rights, including the right to *life*. How did our country wander so far from its noble beginnings, to the point where abortion has morphed from a crime to a fundamental constitutional right?

## From the Bedroom to the Courtroom: The Right To Do Wrong

The highly debated 1973 *Roe v. Wade* decision did not happen in a vacuum. Earlier decisions about privacy set the stage. In 1965, two doctors were criminally convicted as accessories for providing medical advice to married persons on how to prevent conception using a contraceptive device. Contraception was a crime under Connecticut law. The Supreme Court struck down this law, reasoning that the Constitution guaranteed a "zone of privacy" protecting individuals from government intrusion into their private lives.[5] Although the statute had a valid purpose in regulating sexual promiscuity—a purpose no longer likely to withstand legal challenge—it was considered too broad and intrusive. The Court found that the law unconstitutionally interfered with the right to marital privacy.

Privacy in the marital bedroom may seem uncontroversial. But seven years later, the Court took the "right to privacy" to the next level. In Massachusetts, a man was convicted for giving a contraceptive foam to a *single* student after a lecture about contraception. The Supreme Court struck down the applicable statute because it distinguished between married and single persons in violation of the Equal Protection Clause of the Fourteenth Amendment.[6]

This time, the Court found that deterring fornication was not a proper purpose. The "right to privacy" was deemed an *individual* right rather than the right of a married couple. The ruling essentially established a right to sexual promiscuity, although it did not expressly say so:

> If the right of privacy means anything, it is the right of the *individual*, married or single, to be free from unwarranted governmental intrusion into matters so fundamentally affecting a person as the decision whether to bear or beget a child.[7]

Meanwhile, another disastrous decision helped pave the road to *Roe*. Dr. Vuitch was indicted for violation of a statute in the District of Columbia that prohibited abortion unless necessary to preserve the life or health of the mother. He challenged the statute, claiming the term health was too vague.[8] The Supreme Court upheld the law because health was adequately defined in earlier cases. But unfortunately, the word *health* was read broadly to encompass *psychological* as well as physical health dangers. That opened the door for all sorts of subjective interpretations and justifications for taking the life of a child in the womb.

Then came the bombshell. The Supreme Court shredded years of precedent and erased state laws all over America when justices decided *Roe v. Wade* in 1973.[9] A single pregnant woman challenged existing Texas law, which prohibited abortion unless necessary to save the mother's life. This poorly reasoned landmark case established a qualified right for a woman to terminate her pregnancy:

(1) in consultation with her doctor during the first trimester,

(2) subject to state regulation to protect her health during the second trimester, and

(3) subject to stricter legal scrutiny—even prohibition—during the third and final trimester (after viability), in order to protect the baby's *potential* human life or the mother's life or health. The Court determined that liberty includes personal, marital, familial, *and sexual privacy*, specifically, the right not to suffer the distress of bearing and caring for an unwanted child. As in *Vuitch*, the Court recognized imminent psychological harm as justification for abortion.

The Court also decided a companion case from Georgia filed by a woman who was pregnant, poor, abandoned by her husband, and a mental patient. Here, the Court set aside accreditation requirements for institutions performing abortions, and advance approval by an abortion committee,[10] concluding that "childbirth may deprive a woman of her preferred lifestyle and force upon her a radically different and undesired future."[11]

*Terminating the life of an unborn child—previously defined as a criminal act—was thus transformed into a constitutional right.*

The *Roe* court, amazingly, declared that "we need not resolve the difficult question of when life begins,"[12] but that is exactly what they did. The Court bolstered its opinion with an extensive discussion of Greek and Roman law, ancient religion, the Hippocratic Oath, Greek philosophers (Plato and Aristotle), common law, Christian theologians (Augustine and Aquinas), early American legal commentators (Coke and Blackstone), and legal developments in England.[13] The Court then justified its creation of the novel right to abortion with the observation that many state criminal abortion laws were not enacted until the latter half of the 19th century.

The alleged right to privacy admittedly does not include an absolute, unrestricted right to do whatever a person desires with his/her own body. Courts have upheld mandatory vaccination laws.[14] Moreover, pregnancy is not equivalent to other privacy rights because another life—at least a potential life as the Court describes it—is involved.[15] However, in complete disregard for the fundamental right to be born alive, the Court manufactured a right to abortion by exalting the inconvenience and costs associated with bringing a child into the world:

> Maternity, or additional offspring, may force upon the woman a distressful life and future. Psychological harm may be imminent. Mental and physical health may be taxed by childcare. There is also the distress, for all concerned, associated with the unwanted child, and there is the problem of bringing a child into a family already unable, psychologically and otherwise, to care for it. In other cases, as in this one, the additional

difficulties and continuing stigma of unwed motherhood may be involved.[16]

This is a shocking and warped description of motherhood.

The Court also looked to existing laws to distinguish abortion from outright murder. State laws typically would not charge the *woman* as an accomplice. Only the physician was subject to criminal charges. Penalties for criminal abortion were normally much less severe than those prescribed for murder. Moreover, abortion statutes normally contained exceptions for the life of the mother.[17] But saving the mother's life is comparable to self defense. Existing laws don't necessarily reflect a correct understanding of personhood, which does not depend upon either statutory or judicial decree. Many racially discriminatory laws required substantial revision in order to comport with a proper view of *persons* entitled to constitutional protection. Even the U.S. Constitution had to be amended to ensure its full application to citizens of all races.

After countless intervening decisions, the Supreme Court took on the watershed *Casey* case in 1992.[18] Five provisions of the Pennsylvania Abortion Control Act were challenged, with mixed results. The Court rejected the rigid trimester framework it had created in *Roe*, but refused to overrule *Roe's* central holding:

- the woman's right to abort before viability,
- the State's power to restrict abortion after viability,
- the State's interest in protecting the woman's health,
- "and the life of the fetus that may become a child" throughout the pregnancy.[19]

The *Casey* decision is extraordinarily lengthy and detailed. The Court proclaimed that while abortion is morally offensive to some of us: "Our obligation is to define the liberty of all, not to mandate our own moral code."[20] This doublespeak ignores the obvious fact that the law necessarily mandates someone's moral code. The opinion justifies abortion as a choice, "central to personal dignity and autonomy,"[21] disclaiming responsibility for the consequences in this often-quoted statement:

At the heart of liberty is the right to define one's own concept of existence, of meaning, of the universe, and of the mystery of human life. Beliefs about these matters could not define the attributes of personhood were they formed under compulsion of the State.[22]

The upshot of all the *Casey* Court's irrational rhetoric was the creation of a brand new undue burden standard for laws regulating abortion. A state regulation would be invalid if it had "the purpose or effect of placing a substantial obstacle in the path of a woman seeking an abortion of a nonviable fetus."[23] The result is that abortion receives far greater legal protection than religious freedom, which—as we saw in Chapter 3—can be easily overridden by a "neutral law of general applicability."

## Children, Choices, and Challenges

*Roe* was followed by a barrage of state statutes designed to limit its deadly impact: informed consent by the woman seeking an abortion, waiting periods, spousal consent or notice, parental consent or notice for minor females, reporting requirements, funding limitations, requirements that doctors exercise due care for the baby's life, second physician and licensed facility requirements, advertising restrictions, and laws targeting specific procedures such as "partial birth" abortion. Challenges and court decisions quickly followed. Litigation opportunities swelled when, three years after *Roe*, the Supreme Court held that physicians and clinics may challenge abortion restrictions on behalf of their female patients.[24]

## Viability and Liability

Viability is a critical milestone during pregnancy. The *Roe* Court observed that physicians and their scientific colleagues have generally discarded the religious concept of quickening in favor of a focus on conception, live birth, and viability, "the interim point at which the fetus becomes . . . potentially able to live outside the mother's womb."[25] Viability is legally important because it marks the point at which states may enact laws to protect the unborn child. A physician's liability may hinge on compliance with laws requiring a determination of viability prior to abortion, and/or laws requiring the exercise of due care for a viable unborn child. But "viability" has sparked many legal challenges. Unfortunately, the abortion "right" has become so sacred that both women and their doctors escape legal liability for the terminating the lives of unborn children.

The Supreme Court has repeatedly invalidated laws requiring doctors to exercise care for the life of the unborn. Three years after *Roe*, the Court upheld Missouri's definition of viability as the potential ability of the baby to survive outside the mother's womb. But the Court invalidated a state law requiring doctors to exercise professional care for the unborn child's life and health because it did not exclude the time period prior to viability.[26] In 1979, the Court struck down a Pennsylvania law requiring a doctor to exercise care to preserve the life and health of a *viable* unborn child, according to the same standard as if no abortion were intended.[27] The doctor was also required to utilize an abortion technique most likely to ensure the baby would be born alive. Unfortunately, the Court found this law "too vague" because viability is a medical concept that may vary with each pregnancy. Moreover, the viability requirement might discourage couples wanting to abort a deformed child. The law also had a potentially *chilling effect* on the willingness of doctors to perform abortions, because they might be liable for failing to exercise due care. In the mid–1980's, the Court invalidated a similar Pennsylvania regulation requiring that, if a viable fetus were aborted, the doctor must provide the best opportunity for the child to be born alive. This standard of care increased the mother's risk in order to save the baby, and the Court found such a "trade-off" to be *undesirable*.

In a more life-affirming decision, the Supreme Court (1979) reversed a lower court's order that a doctor who aborted a twenty-five-week old fetus could not be prosecuted.[28] The reversal was based on the Court's previously approved definition of viability (*Colautti*) as merely the *potential* rather than *actual* ability to live outside the womb. The expanded definition allowed for the possibility of prosecuting the doctor.

In 1989, the Court once again considered Missouri's abortion laws. This time it upheld several provisions, including a preamble stating that life begins at conception and unborn children have all the legal rights of other citizens.[29] The law required medical testing to determine viability in pregnancies of twenty weeks or more, including measures of gestational age, weight, and lung maturity. This decision was more encouraging than many others were, because the Court affirmed that a state may choose to enact laws that favor childbirth.

*Casey* (1992) revisited the issue of viability, affirming that landmark as the earliest point where the state may regulate nontherapeutic abortions but rejecting the rigid definition of viability formulated under *Roe's* trimester scheme. Justice Scalia dissented from the majority opinion and criticized the arbitrariness of the viability line. Pinpointing a "magical second" when the unborn child's life merits protection "makes no more sense than according infants legal protection only after the point when they can feed themselves."[30]

## Uninformed Consent

It's common practice to require informed consent before a medical procedure. But when it comes to abortion, such consent is anything but routine. Abortion activists describe themselves as pro-*choice* but are often inclined to withhold critical information that might discourage that choice.

Three years after *Roe*, the Supreme Court reached the reasonable conclusion that a state may require a woman to sign a form stating that her consent was informed, freely given, and not the product of coercion.[31] But two cases in the 1980s cast a dark shadow over informed consent requirements. First, the Court struck down a city ordinance in Akron, Ohio, requiring certain disclosures to ensure informed consent, including information about fetal development, potential complications, and alternatives to abortion. The physician was also required to inform the woman that the unborn child is a human being from the moment of conception. These disclosures were considered too extensive, intruding on the doctor's discretion and improperly persuading women against abortions. The Court also struck down a mandatory twenty-four hour waiting period.[32] Similarly, the Court invalidated a provision in the Pennsylvania Abortion Control Act of 1982 that required disclosures about fetal development, medical risks, availability of agencies to assist with childbirth, the father's financial responsibilities, and detrimental psychological effects. The Court objected to "regulations designed to influence the woman's informed choice between abortion or childbirth."[33]

The tide has since turned in a more favorable direction. The 1992 *Casey* decision, despite its many flaws, expressly overruled portions of *Akron* and *Thornburgh* and approved requirements to provide truthful, non-misleading information:

> To the extent *Akron I* and *Thornburgh* find a constitutional violation when the government requires, as it does here, the giving of truthful, nonmisleading information about the nature of the procedure, the attendant health risks and those of childbirth, and the "probable gestational age" of the fetus, those cases go too far, are inconsistent with *Roe's* acknowledgment of an important interest in potential life, and are overruled.[34]

More recently, the Supreme Court made important findings about informed consent in its decision upholding the Federal Partial-Birth Abortion Ban of 2003. The Court observed that "abortion is a 'difficult and painful moral decision,' and thus it seems unexceptionable to conclude some women come to regret their choice to abort the infant life they once created and sustained."[35] Consequently, the state may reasonably enact laws to ensure that women are well-informed, particularly where gruesome partial-birth procedures are performed:

> It is self-evident that a mother who comes to regret her choice to abort must struggle with grief more anguished and sorrow more profound when she learns, only after the event, what she once did not know: that she allowed a doctor to pierce the skull and vacuum the fast-developing brain of her unborn child, a child assuming the human form.[36]

## Parental Bypass

Abortion rights were originally grounded in the "right to privacy" in *family* matters, but court decisions have significantly eroded parental authority in the home. Parents have the right to control the upbringing of their children but can be summarily excluded from a minor daughter's decision to abort her child. Courts have upheld parental notice and consent statutes *only* where the law contains "judicial bypass" provisions allowing young girls to obtain abortions with the consent of a judge instead their parents. These court rulings bypass parental rights in order to preserve a minor female's fundamental right to abort her unborn child.

Shortly after *Roe*, states began enacting laws to protect minor females by requiring parental notice or consent. An onslaught of court challenges ensued, and several reached the Supreme Court. Three years after *Roe*, the Court invalidated a Missouri regulation requiring a girl under age eighteen to obtain the consent of at least one parent, because minors are protected by the Constitution and *no third party* should be given veto power.[37] Shortly thereafter, the Court invalidated a two-parent consent requirement and established the standard that has generally been followed ever since.[38] Courts consider an absolute third party veto unconstitutional, *but* parental consent can be required so long as there is a "judicial bypass" procedure that meets the following criteria:

1. The minor must be allowed to demonstrate her maturity to make the decision to have an abortion;
2. The minor must be allowed to show that parental notification is not in her best interests, even if she lacks the maturity to make the decision herself;
3. The procedure must ensure the minor's anonymity;
4. The procedure must be conducted in a timely manner.

Litigation did not come to an end. Supreme Court battles still erupted and statutes were tested by the *Bellotti* standard, with mixed results:

- The Court upheld a Utah parental notice statute over the objections of an unmarried 15-year-old, noting that states may encourage a minor to consult with her parents in the grave decision concerning abortion.[39]
- The Court struck down an Ohio statute requiring parental consent because it lacked a judicial bypass provision and considered all minors under age 15 too immature to make the decision to abort.[40]
- The Court upheld a Missouri parental consent statute with a judicial bypass provision. The state could only deny an abortion to a minor not mature enough to make her own decision.[41]
- The Court invalidated a Minnesota two-parent notification requirement, because it lacked a judicial bypass procedure and might have harmful effects in cases of divorce or households where domestic violence was present.[42]
- The Court upheld an Ohio requirement to notify one parent or obtain a judicial waiver, rejecting an abortion clinic's argument that the judicial procedure was too burdensome.[43]
- The landmark *Casey* decision, similarly, upheld a one-parent notice requirement that contained judicial bypass provisions.[44]
- The Court upheld a parental notice statute in Montana, because the minor had the opportunity to show that parental notification would not be in her best interests.[45]

In 2006, the Supreme Court upheld New Hampshire's Parental Notification Prior to Abortion Act and remanded for further consideration, reversing a lower court decision to invalidate the entire Act. The law required forty-eight hours written notice to a minor's parent prior to abortion. Three abortion clinics and one obstetrician-gynecologist had challenged the Act.

It's unsettling to observe that so many cases over the years have challenged the rights of parents to even receive notice of their young daughter's intent to abort her child, let alone grant permission. States have attempted to alleviate the harsh results of *Roe* by protecting minors but have only achieved partial success.

## Dad's "Right to Choose"?

The right of a woman to choose has been highly exalted. But what about dad? Does the father have any right to determine that his child will be born over the objections of the mother who wants to abort? In *Roe v. Wade*, the Supreme Court declined to consider whether an unborn child's father had any legal rights. Three years later, the Court held that it was unconstitutional to give veto power to *any* third party, whether a spouse (the father) or even a court.[46] Several years later, a father in Indiana applied for a court order to prevent the mother from aborting their child. Although the Court gave lip service to balancing the rights of father and mother, this particular couple was not married, would probably never reunite, and the father already had other children. His romantic life was unstable, and the child to be aborted was the product of a brief affair. The Supreme Court found no reason to override the mother's decision to have an abortion.[47]

The 1992 *Casey* decision seems to shed a ray of light on the issue, concluding that "a husband's interests in procreation within marriage and in the potential life of his unborn child are certainly substantial ones."[48] But that same case invalidated a Pennsylvania law requiring a woman to notify her husband of her intention to have an abortion, because that would impose a substantial obstacle likely to prevent a significant number of women from obtaining abortions.[49] The Court expressly rejected the view from earlier times that the woman is the center of home and family life, and found that the decision to abort weighs in favor of her wishes in the event of a disagreement between husband and wife.[50]

Biblically, the *husband (father)* is the head of the home (Eph. 5:22–33). Judicial decisions about abortion over the past few decades have reversed the roles of father and mother in the home by exalting the *mother's* right to abort her child. But this intrusion on the privacy of family life receives no attention from the courts.

## Physicians and Facilities

Some challenged laws are intended to regulate the persons who perform abortions and the institutions where the procedure takes place. Such laws are generally a valid means to protect the mother's health and life.

The state may properly regulate the qualifications of persons performing abortions. A Connecticut anti-abortion statute was upheld as applied to a person not licensed as a physician.[51] Similarly, years later the Court upheld a Montana law requiring that a licensed physician perform an abortion. No "undue burden" existed since there was only *one* licensed non-physician in the state performing abortions. The Court refused to attribute improper motives to the legislators, even though an anti-abortion group had drafted the law.[52] But the Court refused to uphold a Pennsylvania statute requiring the presence of a *second* physician in post-viability abortions for non-emergency abortions.[53]

Hospitalization requirements have been challenged with mixed results. Three Supreme Court cases addressed the issue in 1983. First, the Court invalidated an Ohio requirement for hospitalization in a full-service, acute care facility for abortions after the first trimester. This was deemed a heavy and unnecessary burden on the right to abort because it was very costly and might require travel to locate a qualified facility, and thus presented a "significant obstacle."[54] Similarly, the Court struck down a Missouri statute requiring hospitalization in an acute care facility for abortions after twelve weeks of pregnancy. That law was also considered an undue burden on the right to abortion.[55] Nevertheless, the Court upheld the conviction of a Virginia doctor who unlawfully performed an abortion outside a licensed facility during the second trimester of a pregnancy. The state may mandate hospitalization during the later stages of pregnancy to protect the woman's health and life.[56]

The amazing thing about these cases is that they actually reached the highest court in our land. Statutes requiring licensed doctors and hospitals would seem to be routine precautions to protect a pregnant woman's life and health, not a controversial burden on abortion. Abortion proponents remind us of the back-alley, dangerous abortions performed prior to *Roe v. Wade*, but demand that courts invalidate statutes requiring properly licensed doctors and safe facilities.

## "Fundamental" Right to Funding?

Abortion has become enshrined in our judicial system as a *fundamental* constitutional right. But does it include *entitlement* to government funding? Does it override a state policy that expressly favors life? The answer to that question may be changing as this book goes to press. The proposed national health care system and the "Freedom of Choice Act" both threaten to establish entitlement to public funding for those who cannot afford abortions.

Past court decisions hold that a state may choose to encourage childbirth, and the government is not required to finance abortions. State Medicaid funding need not cover abortion. Under Title XIX of the Social Security Act, states may choose whether or not to fund non-therapeutic abortions.[57] States may finance childbirth without being obligated to fund abortions. In 1980, the Supreme Court upheld the Hyde Amendment to the Social Security Act, which restricts federal funding of Medicaid abortions to cases where the mother's life is endangered.[58] The Hyde Amendment was later revised to require that states participating in Medicaid must fund abortions in rape or incest cases. Consequently, the Supreme Court struck down an Arkansas constitutional amendment that prohibited the use of public funds for abortions except where necessary to save the mother's life.[59]

In a favorable, frequently quoted decision, the Supreme Court validated Title X of the Public Health Service Act, which authorized government grants and contracts to assist in family planning projects but banned financing of programs where "abortion is a method of family planning."[60] The government may value childbirth over abortion and allocate its funds accordingly. Women are not denied the right to choose abortion merely because the state refuses to finance the procedure.

States are also not required to get into the abortion business. In 1977, the Supreme Court upheld a policy set by the mayor of St. Louis to prohibit abortions in city hospitals except in cases involving serious threat to the mother's life or health.[61] A few years later, the Court upheld Missouri statutes that prohibited public employees from participating in non-emergency abortions and forbade the use of public funds to counsel or encourage abortion.[62]

There are other, more subtle dangers in laws not directly related to abortion regulation. The California Supreme Court ruled against a religious charity opposed to contraception by requiring it to include contraceptives in its prescription drug program for employees, under the California Women's Contraception Equity Act.[63] The narrowly drafted exception for religious organizations was not broad enough to cover this charity that had to abandon the program for all employees or violate its religious convictions.

A constitutional right is not an entitlement. Americans have the right to free speech but cannot expect the government to pay for the paper and ink. Moreover, considering the controversial moral nature of abortion, pro-life taxpayers should not be required to indirectly provide funding for it. But there is grave danger on the horizon as President Obama's national health care program is debated.

## Partial Birth—Total Death

Late-term, *partial birth* abortions are particularly gruesome, highlighting the reality that abortion is infanticide. Courts have split hairs over the language in laws prohibiting partial birth abortion. There are good decisions and bad ones, but the most recent cases are encouraging.

In one of the first partial birth abortion cases, clinics and doctors sued to enjoin enforcement of the Virginia Partial Birth Abortion Act. The Act prohibited partial birth abortions not necessary to save the mother's life and outlawed a procedure involving rupture of the baby's skull and sucking out its contents. More specifically, the law prohibited the deliberate and intentional delivery of an intact living baby into the vagina for the purpose of performing a procedure to kill that fetus. The Fourth Circuit Federal Court of Appeals found the law was valid and rejected arguments that it was too vague.[64]

Unfortunately, in the same year (1998) the Seventh Circuit Court of Appeals struck down a Wisconsin statute that imposed life imprisonment for the performance of a partial birth abortion (dilation & extract or D&E) unless necessary to save the mother's life. This federal court held that the law imposed a substantial burden on the right to abortion because there was no exception for the mother's *health*, no exception for a fetus not yet viable, and the law was too vague in its "sweeping prohibition" of the procedure.[65] A couple of years later, the Supreme Court rendered a similar decision when it invalidated a Nebraska statute that criminalized performance of a partial birth abortion, defined as "deliberately and intentionally delivering into the vagina a living unborn child, or a substantial portion thereof, for the purpose of performing a procedure that the person performing such procedure knows will kill the unborn child and does kill the unborn child."[66] The prohibition was deemed an undue burden because the law had no exception to preserve the mother's *health*. Its only exception was danger to the mother's *life*. Following this case (*Stenberg*), Illinois and Wisconsin both conceded that their partial birth abortion statutes imposed an unconstitutional undue burden on abortion rights because there was no health exception.

There is a glimmer of light at the end of this tunnel. Congress passed the federal Partial Birth Abortion Act of 2003, and the Supreme Court upheld it in early 2007.[67] It's not too vague, nor does it impose an undue burden. To violate the Act, a doctor must knowingly and intentionally perform an act, other than delivery, that kills the partially delivered baby after it has been delivered to an anatomical landmark. Congressional findings included statements that pro-life advocates can applaud:

> Implicitly approving such a brutal and inhumane procedure by choosing not to prohibit it will further coarsen society to the humanity of not only newborns, but all vulnerable and innocent human life, making it increasingly difficult to protect such life.[68]
>
> Partial-birth abortion . . . confuses the medical, legal, and ethical duties of physicians to preserve and promote life, as the physician acts directly against the physical life of a child, whom he or she had just delivered, all but the head, out of the womb, in order to end that life."[69]

Congress concluded that the abortion methods it proscribed had a disturbing similarity to the killing of a newborn infant, and thus acted to draw a bright line that would clearly distinguish abortion from infanticide.[70]

The Richmond Medical Center recently made headlines again, when the Fourth Circuit upheld the Virginia Partial Birth Infanticide Act passed in 2003. That Act prohibits killing a human infant who has been completely or substantially expelled or extracted from its mother, meaning that its entire head is outside the mother's body, or, in the case of a breech delivery, its trunk past the navel is outside. Judge Wilkinson's comments, concurring in the opinion, are encouraging:

> How a society treats its most vulnerable members may do more than grandiosity to shape its lasting worth. A partially born child is among the weakest, most helpless beings in our midst and on that account exerts a special claim on our protection. . . . The fact is that we—civilized people—are retreating to the haven of our Constitution to justify dismembering a partly born child and crushing its skull. Surely centuries hence, people will look back on this gruesome practice done in the name of fundamental law by a society of high achievement. And they will shudder.[71]

## Right to Life—Right to Death

Life and death legal battles now extend from the womb to the tomb. The sanctity of life derives from the biblical fact that human beings are created in the image of God (Genesis 1:27–28). Abortionists deny sanctity at the beginning of life, and a similar disrespect for life now surrounds the end of life. The right to *death* seemingly trumps the right to *life*.

After an automobile accident, Nancy Cruzan was in a coma with virtually no chance of recovery. Her husband kept her alive artificially, but her parents asked that life support be withdrawn. Missouri law required clear and convincing evidence of a comatose person's desire to withdraw life support, and Cruzan's casual conversation with a friend did not meet that standard. The Supreme Court upheld the state law because it guarded against potential abuses, carefully noting the distinction between suicide assistance and allowing a natural death by withdrawal of artificial support. There are differences in intent—to cause death, or to honor the patient's wishes—and in causation—the underlying disease, or actively lethal means such as medication.[72]

Years later, Terry Schiavo's life-and-death ordeal made national headlines, commanding the attention of courts, legislatures, and media. This time it was the husband wanting to withdraw life support, while her parents fought for her life. Their legal struggle was ultimately unsuccessful and she passed away.[73]

Assisted suicide statutes have been the subject of two Supreme Court cases. In 1997, the Court upheld a Washington statute providing that willful suicide assistance is a felony.[74] The Constitution protects fundamental liberties that are deeply rooted in our nation's history, but the right to commit suicide is not one of these. More recently, the Court invalidated an interpretive rule issued by the U.S. Attorney General that would have frustrated implementation of the Oregon Death with Dignity Act. The rule determined that using controlled substances to assist a suicide was not a legitimate medical practice and therefore violated the federal Controlled Substances Act. The split Court held that the Attorney General did not have the power to declare illegitimate a medical standard that was specifically authorized by state law.

Rights to abortion and to refuse life-saving medical treatment are both based on autonomy, the right to control one's own body. But the Bible has a different message for believers, who were bought at a price—the precious blood of Christ—and therefore belong to Him (1 Cor. 6:19–20; Gal. 2:20; 1 Pet. 1:18–19). Not that human life must always, in all circumstances and at all costs, be artificially preserved indefinitely—but at the very least, end-of-life decisions require extreme caution, always remembering that God is the author of life. He knows the number of our days and has ordained each one of them (Ps. 139:16).

## Onward Christian Soldiers

Abortion is an explosive topic that inflames passions on both sides. The controversy has not subsided in the nearly four decades since *Roe v. Wade*. It's encouraging to note a recent pro-life movement to pass state laws and constitutional amendments defining personhood in a biblical manner and thus protect the unborn child's right to life.[75] In July 2009, Colorado and Montana officially launched personhood amendments and petitions that will be going out for signatures. But there is much work to be done. The length of this chapter, and the number of court decisions parsing every conceivable sort of statute, testifies to the strength of the battle—and we have barely scratched the surface.

# Judicial Suicide:
# Unraveling the
# Constitution

*A man's own folly ruins his life, but his heart rages against the Lord* (PROVERBS 19:3 NIV).

> The Christian Legal Society was busy in court during 2006, as student chapters in Illinois and California faced loss of university recognition and benefits for discriminating on the basis of religion and sexual orientation. But discrimination cuts both ways. The Christian students face charges of discrimination and intolerance but they're victims of that same evil. As the winds of political correctness shift, the perpetrators and victims of discrimination will switch positions.

iberal activists have gained substantial legal ground through the exercise of basic constitutional rights, including free speech, press, association, and the political process. But in denying religious liberty to opponents who don't wish to facilitate or participate in their agenda, they shred the U. S. Constitution—*the very document that enabled them to establish their current legal rights.* Under the guise of tolerance for a variety of lifestyles and behaviors, this deadly double standard threatens the constitutional rights of all Americans. Aggressive activists actually threaten their own civil rights in the process of denying Christians the right to practice their faith.

Similarly, other logical inconsistencies stretch the Constitution to the breaking point as activists manufacture novel new rights like abortion and sexual immorality. The Constitution will be nothing more than confetti if this trend continues.

## Crushing Their Own Foundation

Homosexuals have acquired unprecedented new legal rights, including the right to be free of discrimination based on their sexual orientation—and recently, even the right to marry persons of the same sex in a few states. They have accomplished this dramatic social and political change by using the political process and exercising their constitutional rights, such as free speech and association. But overly aggressive assertion of such rights threatens to erode the liberties of all Americans. When they shred the Constitution as it applies to Christians, activists simultaneously threaten to extinguish their own rights.

Even sympathetic commentators acknowledge that homosexuals cannot demand for themselves what they would deny to others. Their rights are not superior to those of everyone else.[1] Some even recognize the intrusion on religious liberties: "In some instances, full gay equality would be a fundamental affront to liberty interests of religious or traditionalist groups, in ways that full gender or race equality no longer are."[2]

Courts need to preserve the constitutional liberties guaranteed to *all* citizens. Americans who want to guard their own civil rights must respect their opponents rather than crushing them with debilitating legal penalties:

> The price of freedom of religion or of speech or of the press is that we must put up with, and even pay for, a good deal of rubbish.[3]

If Americans are going to preserve their civil liberties . . . they will need to develop thicker skin. One price of living in a free society is toleration of those who intentionally or unintentionally offend others. The current trend, however, is to give offended parties a legal remedy, as long as the offense can be construed as discrimination. . . . Preserving liberalism, and the civil liberties that go with it, requires a certain level of virtue by the citizenry. Among those necessary virtues is tolerance of those who intentionally or unintentionally offend, and sometimes, when civil liberties are implicated, who blatantly discriminate. A society that undercuts civil liberties in pursuit of the "equality" offered by a statutory right to be free from all slights will ultimately end up with neither equality nor civil liberties.[4]

Christians must endure numerous offenses, including profanity and media images that border on pornography. The First Amendment protects these forms of expression, however offensive they may be. Yet advocates of alternate lifestyles believe they're entitled to be free of all religious objections to their agenda, and they don't hesitate to utilize the judicial system to silence believers.

Some court decisions threaten to dismantle religious liberty in order to promote political agendas that are deeply troubling to many Americans. America's founders risked their lives to escape religious tyranny and observe their faith free from government intrusion. Congress has ranked religious freedom "among the most treasured birthrights of every American."[5] The U. S. Supreme Court expressed it eloquently in ruling that an alien could not be denied citizenship because of his religious objections to bearing arms:

The struggle for religious liberty has through the centuries been an effort to accommodate the demands of the State to the conscience of the individual. The victory for freedom of thought recorded in our Bill of Rights recognizes that in the domain of conscience there is a moral power higher than the State. Throughout the ages, men have suffered death rather than subordinate their allegiance to God to the authority of the State. Freedom of religion guaranteed by the First Amendment is the product of that struggle.[6]

We dare not sacrifice our priceless American freedoms in pursuit of the free exercise of sexuality, yet there is an ominous trend in that direction. If it continues and succeeds, *all* Americans will suffer the loss of basic liberties.

## Deadly Double Standards

In 1987, a federal court required a Catholic university in the District of Columbia to extend tangible benefits to a homosexual student group.[7] Twenty years later, as we saw in Chapter 4, public law schools in California and Illinois fought battles in federal court to avoid granting similar benefits to student chapters of the Christian Legal Society because of their discriminatory policies. Something is horribly wrong when a religious institution must recognize a group organized around sexual immorality but a religious student group is denied benefits available to all other student groups—including funds, facilities, and mass communication with students—because it adheres to its own religious standards and refuses to admit openly practicing homosexuals.

The California federal court attempted to distinguish the *Hurley* case, where the Supreme Court held that parade organizers were not required to include a gay-rights marching unit in their St. Patrick's Day parade. The parade did not exclude all *individual* gay, lesbian, or bisexual persons from marching in approved parade units, but the District Court conveniently overlooked the CLS policy to welcome all students at its meetings and activities. Only members and leaders were required to affirm a statement of faith and refrain from openly immoral conduct such as homosexuality.

Under similar facts, CLS fared better in the Seventh Circuit Court of Appeals, an appellate court that is higher up the federal ladder than the District Court in San Francisco. Christian students at Southern Illinois University School of Law organized a CLS chapter but were denied official recognition because of their discriminatory policies. The favorable appellate ruling was based on the constitutional rights to free speech and association. This court rightly recognized that forced acceptance of homosexual members and leaders would threaten the very existence of the organization:

CLS is a faith-based organization. One of its beliefs is that sexual conduct outside of a traditional marriage is immoral. It would be difficult for CLS to sincerely and effectively convey a message of disapproval of certain types of conduct if, at the same time, it must accept members who engage in that conduct. CLS's beliefs about sexual morality are among its defining values; forcing it to accept as members those who engage in or approve of homosexual conduct would cause the group as it currently identifies itself to cease to exist.[8]

This is a reasonable, commonsense, morally sound conclusion. *However, it's distressing that Christian law students had to engage in protracted litigation in our federal courts and wait for an appellate court to vindicate their right to organize a CLS chapter on campus.* Moreover, these two law schools violated their own policies. They discriminated against the Christian students on the basis of religion—one of their own protected categories—by refusing to recognize the CLS chapters.

## It's a Boy—It's a Girl—It's a *Child*

Justice Scalia observed in his *Casey* dissent that: "'[R]easoned judgment' does not begin by begging the question, as *Roe* and subsequent cases unquestionably did by assuming that what the State is protecting is mere 'potentiality of human life.'"[9]

*Roe, Doe, Casey,* and other abortion decisions have a glaring internal inconsistency that is like the proverbial elephant in the room or the naked emperor who marches down the street while onlookers ignore his lack of clothing. All of these decisions presuppose that the so-called "fetus" is a *child*, exalting the right to abort the fetus *because it is a child* while simultaneously—but inconsistently—denying its humanity. The abortion right is incoherent without the assumption that the fetus *is a child*. Yet it also rests on the assumption that the fetus *is not a child* but merely a *potential* life. Abortionists and their judicial allies speak from both sides of their mouths when they assert a right that rests on two mutually exclusive assumptions. The *Roe* decision admitted that its legal foundation would collapse if the personhood of the fetus were established, "for the fetus life would then be guaranteed specifically by the [Fourteenth] Amendment."[10] What the Court did not see—or would not openly admit—is that it presupposes the very personhood it denies. A few pages after this admission, the Court refers to its 1972 *Eisenstadt* case, which holds that an individual should be free of government intrusion in such private matters "as the decision whether to bear or beget a *child*."[11] Yes, a *child* is not a piece of tissue, not a tumor, not a monkey, or a cat, or a dog—but a *child*. It's the burden and responsibility of bearing and raising a *child* that women wish to avoid by having abortions:

> Certainly the interests of a woman in giving of her physical and emotional self during pregnancy and the interests that will be affected throughout her life by the birth and raising of a *child* are of a far greater degree of significance and personal intimacy than the right to send a child to private school protected in *Pierce v. Society of Sisters, 268 U.S. 510 (1925)*, or the right to teach a foreign language protected in *Meyer v. Nebraska, 262 U.S. 390 (1923)*.[12]

Absent a miscarriage—or abortion—the fetus growing inside the womb of its mother will inevitably emerge as a human *child*, not a piece of tissue or some other life form. If there were any chance that the fetus might be *something other than a child*, the heart of the abortion right would crumble. There would be no reason to passionately lobby for the right to abort the fetus if it were anything but a *child*, a *person* who will demand the mother's physical, emotional, and financial resources during the birth process and years beyond. *The right to abortion is essentially the right to avoid the responsibilities of motherhood.*

Other cases follow suit. The companion *Doe* case lamented the hardships of pregnancy, because women are required to:

> . . . endure the discomforts of pregnancy; to incur the pain, higher mortality rate, and aftereffects of *childbirth*; to abandon educational plans; to sustain loss of income; to forgo the satisfactions of careers to tax further mental and physical health

in providing *child* care; and, in some cases, to bear the lifelong stigma of unwed motherhood, a badge which may haunt, if not deter, later legitimate family relationships.[13]

The burdens described above are related solely to bearing and raising a *child*—never to discarding a piece of tissue, removing a tumor, or caring for non-human forms of life.

The same line of reasoning recurred in the watershed *Casey* decision that described abortion as a unique act with consequences for the mother—pain that only she must bear—plus her spouse, family, society, and "depending on one's beliefs, for the life or potential life that is aborted."[14] The Court admits there are consequences for the fetus but leaves it to the individual imagination whether the unborn is a "life" or merely "potential life, "as if that determination could vary, depending on one's beliefs. In almost the same breath the Court affirms that a state "may express profound respect for the life of the unborn" so long as its laws don't impose a "substantial burden" on abortion rights.[15] So which is it—a life, or only a potential life? And exactly how can a state express profound respect for *life* without substantially burdening the right to terminate life? Moreover, as in earlier cases, *Casey* presupposed the personhood of the unborn child when it explained that:

> Her [the mother's] suffering is too intimate and personal for the State to insist, without more, upon its own vision of the *woman's role*, however dominant that vision has been in the course of our history and our culture. The destiny of the woman must be shaped to a large extent on her own conception of her spiritual imperatives and her place in society.[16]

In an interview with the New York Times in July 2009,[17] a reporter questioned Justice Ruth Bader Ginsburg about *Roe v. Wade* and asked: "Do you see, as part of a future feminist legal wish list, repositioning *Roe* so that the right to abortion is rooted in the constitutional promise of sex equality?" The Justice answered: "Oh, yes, I think it will be." Indeed, she expressed the same view when she dissented from the Supreme Court's 2007 decision upholding the Partial Birth Abortion Act:

[L]egal challenges to undue restrictions on abortion procedures do not seek to vindicate some generalized notion of
privacy; rather, they center on a woman's autonomy to determine her life's course, and thus to enjoy equal citizenship
stature.[18]

Justice Ginsburg calls the Court's defense of the Act "an effort to
chip away at a right declared again and again by the Court—*and
with increasing comprehension of its centrality to women's lives.*"[19] No
repositioning is required. All along, abortion has been touted as a
fundamental right necessary to free women from the alleged burdens of giving birth and raising *children*. If the fetus were anything
other than an unborn *child*, there would be no need to rationalize
abortion by references to sex equality.

## Size, Level of Development, Dependency, Environment—"SLED"

Exposing the logical fallacies of abortion decisions is consistent
with a pro-life argument that does not rely on express references
to religious faith or teachings. The argument is easily remembered
using the acronym "SLED."[20]

**S** is for size: An embryo or unborn child is smaller than a newborn infant. An infant is smaller than a toddler, who is smaller than
an adult, but size does not render the baby any less a person than
a fully grown adult.

**L** is for level of development: The child in the womb is less
developed than a newborn, who in turn is less developed than a
toddler, teen, or adult. But again, personhood does not hinge on the
level of development.

**E** is for environment: The unborn child lives inside the mother's womb, while other persons live outside the mother's body. The
short trip down the birth canal does not magically transform the
essence of the child. If the fetus were something other than a child,
a change in location would not convert it into a human being.

**D** is for degree of dependency: The unborn child depends on
its connection with the mother's body. But what about persons

on kidney dialysis, persons with pacemakers, or persons hooked to oxygen tanks? Personhood is not diminished by such dependence.

These four factors that distinguish the unborn child from a newborn infant—or any other person—are morally irrelevant. Outside the womb, none of them are ever used to measure personhood. Ironically, laws protect the abortion rights of minor females who are smaller and less developed than adult women are.

## Beyond Bizarre

Bizarre arguments abound in abortion decisions. Logic, morality, and legal precedent must all be twisted to manufacture and maintain the *fundamental right* of a mother to abort her child. In *Casey*, the Court asserted that *Roe* could not be overruled because Americans had relied on it for all of about twenty years:

> [F]or two decades of economic and social developments, people have organized intimate relationships and made choices that define their views of themselves and their places in society, *in reliance on the availability of abortion in the event that contraception should fail.* The ability of women to participate equally in the economic and social life of the Nation has been facilitated by their ability to control their reproductive lives.[21]

Under this irrational reasoning, it would appear all but impossible to change *any* law that has been in effect for even a few years. If this rationale were applied to the many laws that *Christians* have relied on for decades—the definition of marriage, for example, and the historically protected freedom to practice one's faith—perhaps we would not be faced with the disastrous legal changes sweeping America today.

## To Bear or *NOT* To Bear

Casting aside logic, the *Casey* Court also asserts that the right to abort is necessary in order to preserve the right *to* bear a child. Without *Roe*, the Court reasoned:

> [T]he State might as readily restrict a woman's right to choose *to* carry a pregnancy to term as to terminate it, to further asserted state interests in population control, or eugenics, for example. Yet *Roe* has been sensibly relied upon to counter any such suggestions.[22]

Again, this argument hinges on the assumption that a *child* is involved. The woman's right *to* bear a *child* allegedly depends on her right *not to* bear a *child*. If the fetus is not a child (a person) this argument lacks coherence. Surely, a woman's right to carry her pregnancy to term and bear a child does not depend on her right to remove a lifeless piece of tissue from her body.

But even with the analogy intact, this argument fails. Sometimes legal rights include the converse. The First Amendment right to free speech encompasses the right not to speak.[23] But this is not inevitably true of every right. The right to life does not depend on the right to commit suicide, as shown by the Court's decision to uphold laws against assisted suicide—laws that protect terminally ill persons from involuntary euthanasia.[24] The right to eat does not depend on the right to starve to death.[25] The right to defend another person's life or health does not include the right to endanger it. Abortion rationale has been stretched well beyond the breaking point.

## Let the Decision Fall

An equally preposterous argument in *Casey* was that *Roe* must stand because of a principle that lawyers call "stare decisis"—literally, "let the decision stand." Courts are reluctant to overrule prior decisions. If they did so frequently, it would create instability and chaos. But while some hesitation is prudent, courts must sometimes overrule clearly erroneous decisions. Sometimes it's wise to let the decision *fall.* That happened in America when the Supreme Court overturned prior cases endorsing racially discriminatory separate but equal provisions. But in *Casey*, the Court steadfastfully refused to admit error, claiming that it would *appear* to be overruling "under fire" from pro-life advocates, and that would tarnish the Court's legitimacy.[26]

Amazingly, the Court cannot even follow its own standards. *Casey* rejected and overruled *Roe's* rigid trimester framework, allowing a major portion of the earlier decision to fall. *Casey* also discarded the Court's previous ruling that a mandatory 24-hour waiting period should be invalidated: "We consider that conclusion to be wrong."[27] Even more perplexing is the opinion's citation to two cases where the Court chose to *depart* from existing precedent—as support for its conclusion that it must continue adherence to *Roe!* The Court cites, for example, the famous 1955 *Brown v. Board of Education* decision that found racial discrimination in public schools unconstitutional.[28] That case struck down an erroneous ruling half a century earlier that mandatory racial segregation in public transportation does not violate the Constitution by treating African-Americans as an inferior race.[29] Similarly, in 1937, the Court signaled the demise of economic autonomy when it upheld a Washington state minimum wage law for women,[30] overturning pre-Depression era cases striking down similar laws regulating working conditions.[31] The Court drastically departed from its earlier precedent when it decided these two landmark cases. It's disingenuous and illogical to cite them as *support* for blind adherence to a twenty-year-old decision creating a novel and highly controversial new right to abort one's own child.

Once again, there are alarming double standards. What would happen if *Casey's* reasoning were applied to homosexual rights? In 2003, the Supreme Court struck down a law that prohibited homosexual sodomy,[32] overruling its 1986 decision that such conduct is not a protected constitutional right—and casting aside a "millennia of moral teaching."[33] Did anyone perhaps rely on the earlier ruling, not to mention centuries of moral teaching? Did anyone question the Court's legitimacy in overruling its own holding from two decades ago? Why is it acceptable to overrule a decision upholding long-established moral standards, but not a decision that created a never-heard-of-before right to abort one's own child?

## Third Party Rights and Fights

Activists argue that the free exercise of religion should not trump *their* rights—freedom from sexual orientation discrimination or the freedom to abort babies. But why should these newly minted rights trump religious liberty? Abortion and sodomy, formerly criminal acts, are now protected rights that trample the right to practice Christianity. Religious liberty is explicitly mentioned and protected by the First Amendment. What is next? Polygamy? Incest? Pedophilia? Bestiality? Necrophilia? Suicide? All of these are similar to abortion and homosexuality because they involve intimate and deeply personal choices about "personal autonomy and bodily integrity."[34] As America wanders further from its Christian roots, these fights over conflicting constitutional rights will only escalate. But if activists successfully trash the First Amendment by trampling religious liberty, there will be no freedom left for anyone.

# Part Two

# Civil Rights:
# Promiscuity, Perversion,
# and Privacy

*Woe to those who call evil good, and good evil; who substitute darkness for light and light for darkness; who substitute bitter for sweet, and sweet for bitter (Isaiah 5:20 NASB).*

The legal system has been turned upside down in recent years. Acts once considered immoral or even criminal—abortion and homosexual sodomy, for example—have morphed into protected civil rights. Opponents may be compelled by law to facilitate their exercise unless there is an applicable statutory exemption in place. Courts in Massachusetts, Iowa, and Connecticut have concocted a constitutional "right" to same-sex marriage, and legislatures in Vermont, Maine, and New Hampshire have followed their lead, shaking the foundation of the American family.

---

*The Vermont legislature overrode the veto of Gov. Jim Douglas to create a statutory right to same-sex marriage, effective September 1, 2009. Maine Gov. John Baldacci signed state legislation on May 6, 2009, scheduled to take effect 90 days after the end of the legislative session in June. Gov. John Lynch signed New Hampshire legislation effective on January 1, 2010, and couples who previously entered into civil unions can apply to have their unions recognized as marriages.

## Seven

# The *Free Exercise*
# of Sexuality

*In those days there was no king in Israel; everyone did what was right in his own eyes* (JUDGES 21:25 ESV).

Lambda Legal is a radical civil rights organization promoting the expansion of legal rights for gay, lesbian, bisexual, and transgender individuals. This group argued that New York City's Administration for Children's Services (ACS) was legally obligated to provide sex reassignment surgery for a transgender eighteen-year-old girl (Mariah, renamed Brian) who had been in the city's care since age ten. The Family Court ordered ACS to provide this allegedly necessary medical treatment, and ACS appealed. New York Supreme Court's First Appellate Division ultimately ruled that the Family Court lacked authority to order ACS to provide the surgery, but it's frightening that a case like this would even reach our courts.[1]

*B*ecause homosexual activism has metastasized, it threatens to rupture the moral fabric of our nation. Like a cancer, it has spread through our society and legal system in a manner that ravages the free exercise of religion, particularly Christianity.

Similarly, abortion is a sacred right, allowing escape from the con-sequences of unrestrained promiscuity. Even modest legal restric-tions, like parental consent or notice for abortions performed on minors, are closely scrutinized by courts.

Pro-homosexual laws lurk behind the covers of state and local law books. A growing number of jurisdictions permit homosex-uals to register as domestic partners and even to adopt children together. An alarming number of states allow same-sex couples to jointly adopt a child.[2] A few other states allow such co-partner adoptions only in certain jurisdictions, rather than state-wide.[3] Many states permit single-parent adoptions through laws that refer to "any adult" without excluding homosexuals.[4] Florida is the only state that explicitly *prohibits* adoption by individual homosexu-als or same-sex couples, although an activist Miami-Dade judge ruled the law unconstitutional in late 2008 and allowed a homo-sexual man to adopt two children who had been living with him since 2004. Mississippi and Utah do not allow same-sex couples to jointly adopt a child.[5]

Homosexuals also enjoy many state and local legal protections from sexual orientation discrimination in housing, employment, education, and public accommodations. There is increasing pres-sure to extend such protection to the federal level, including the Local Law Enforcement Hate Crimes Prevention Act (commonly known as the Matthew Shepard Act), signed into law by President Obama on October 28, 2009,[6] and the Employment Non-Dis-crimination Act (ENDA).[7] Activists have arrogated to themselves the right to redefine the most basic unit of our society—the family. They use our courts and legislatures to wage war against morality and marriage. If you are a Christian operating a business, *or even a ministry*, beware. Your right to practice your faith may be locked behind the doors of your local church sanctuary, and even there it may be at risk. Pro-choice advocates seek unrestrained access to abortion, even if it means overriding the conscience of a doctor, nurse, or pharmacist.

Homosexuals clamor for legal rights, tolerance, and even social approval of an immoral lifestyle, trampling the consciences of those opposed to their agenda. In California public schools, gender has been radically redefined by statute, and it is now illegal for textbooks, teachers, and classes to teach anything that reflects or promotes bias against those with perceived gender issues. This dangerous new legislation (Senate Bill 777) was passed in late 2007, amending numerous sections of the California Education Code. Advocates for Faith and Freedom and the Alliance Defense Fund filed a lawsuit in early 2008 to challenge the law. The plaintiffs are two courageous public school students whose school allows a girl—who self-identifies as a male—to change clothes in the boys locker room.[8]

Great controversy surrounds these divisive moral issues, even within the religious community. When the California Supreme Court considered same-sex marriage issue in 2008, an alarmingly large group of religious organizations filed a brief urging the court to grant them the right to perform same-sex marriage ceremonies. Some of these were Christian groups. We dare not allow recently created statutory and (allegedly) constitutional rights to eviscerate the core constitutional rights of citizens who cannot, in good conscience, subscribe to the politically correct agendas of our times. The distinctly *religious* nature of these controversies is inescapable, and the so-called separation of church and state doctrine can neither resolve nor avoid the issue.

As we saw in Chapter 5, the authors of *Roe v. Wade* discussed the *theological* debates about the beginning point of human life, then arbitrarily answered this *theological* question by setting viability as the point at which the state may regulate abortion.[9] When the California Court of Appeal ruled against same-sex marriage in 2006, one justice observed the "uncomfortable intersection of law, culture, and religion."[10] Homosexual conduct has been condemned for centuries. In 1986 (*Bowers*), U. S. Supreme Court Justice Burger warned that it would "cast aside millennia of moral teaching" to convert it to a fundamental right.[11] Even if such dramatic restructuring of society were appropriate, it should not be coerced through a "subtle, manipulative campaign."[12] Even when overruling the 1986 *Bowers* case that upheld a state law against sodomy, the U. S. Supreme Court acknowledged that:

. . . the Court in *Bowers* was making the broader point that for centuries there have been powerful voices to condemn homosexual conduct as *immoral*. The condemnation has been shaped by *religious* beliefs, conceptions of right and acceptable behavior, and respect for the traditional family. For many persons these are not trivial concerns but profound and deep convictions accepted as ethical and *moral* principles to which they aspire and which thus determine the course of their lives.[13]

The homosexual and pro-choice agendas share similar underpinnings. The right to sexual promiscuity underlies the controversial right to choose to murder a child in the womb, while homosexuals claim the right to practice their perversion—both under the rubric of a right to privacy. Both require the not-so-private assistance of health care professionals. Both attempt to coerce the cooperation of persons who have religious and moral objections to their agenda. Both generate heated moral debate and aggressive political action. Both are rooted in an alleged right to the *free exercise* of sexual sin, pitted against the *free exercise* of religion when opponents are silenced and drafted into contributing personal services to advance the agenda.

God's Word teaches that homosexuality is sin. The Ten Commandments prohibit murder. The civil government does not criminalize all sin, but neither should it be elevated to the status of a civil right that tramples the rights of others to live according to God's law. "We are all sinners. But we all don't demand that our sins be recognized as civil rights."[14]

Homosexuality and abortion are both too morally and legally controversial to justify a severe intrusion on the fundamental liberties of opponents. Many religious citizens abhor the slaughter of unborn children in the womb, however, today's American woman has the liberty to abort her child. Even though homosexual conduct is contrary to centuries of moral and religious teachings, proponents have established novel legal rights and they forge ahead. Alarmed citizens have begun to take action. More than half of the states in America have amended their constitutions to define marriage as the union of one man and one woman.[15]

Colorado and Ohio voters passed initiatives to ban special protections for homosexuals. The Colorado amendment, which banned protected legal status based on sexual orientation, conduct, or relationships, was struck down as overly broad because it imposed a special disability on those persons.[16] A more narrowly drafted Ohio initiative, which prohibited *preferential* treatment, survived judicial review.[17] The very fact that such initiatives were proposed and passed is evidence that Americans are deeply troubled by the homosexual agenda. Nevertheless, it may be too little, too late. Anti-discrimination laws in many states threaten to bulldoze the basic First Amendment liberties of Christians who operate their ministries and businesses according to Scripture. Abortion has long since become an entrenched fundamental right (Chapter 5). States may not place an undue burden in the path of a woman seeking to abort her child.[18] The 2007 Supreme Court decision to uphold the Partial Birth Abortion Act was a step in the right direction, but only a small one. These battles are not over.

## Perilous Precedents

Sexual freedom is not morally comparable to religious freedom. But from a purely legal perspective, some case precedents can be perilous when applied in reverse to silence believers.

In 2006, the U.S. Supreme Court ruled against several law schools that wanted to exclude military recruiters from their campuses because the "don't ask—don't tell" policy conflicted with law school policies prohibiting sexual orientation discrimination.[19] Federal law provides that educational institutions will lose certain funding if they deny equal access to military recruiters.[20] The schools could not continue to receive funds if they enforced their non-discrimination policies protecting homosexuals. The association lost and the schools had to allow the military recruiters access on campus. The mere presence of the recruiters on campus did not violate the law schools' rights to free speech or association, no matter how strongly the schools disagreed with the military message.

The actual result is consistent with Christian values. The law schools could not use their pro-homosexual policies to deny access to military recruiters. But what if this principle were applied in reverse? What if same-sex marriage becomes so widely accepted that individual business owners or organizations have to forego government funding, tax exemptions, or other important benefits in order to avoid coerced association with a reprehensible agenda? The Freedom of Choice Act—currently pushed by the Obama Administration—threatens such results for those who object to abortions. Hospitals, doctors, nurses, and other health care workers may be obliged to either participate in abortion or face the loss of funding, professional certification, and other benefits necessary to remain in business.

## Perilous Political Parallels

Some observers see a parallel between the emerging struggle for gay rights and the battle for religious liberty, arguing that sexual freedom and religious liberty should be conflated so that government attempts to accommodate both—a "live and let live." This is a dangerous tactic that lacks both legal and moral grounding. The First Amendment expressly guarantees religious liberty, whereas sexual liberty must be read into other sections of the Constitution. Moreover, Christians cannot roll over and accommodate sin. Widespread acceptance of same-sex marriage, for example, erodes the very foundation of our society and creates a culture so alien to Christianity that raising children becomes incredibly complicated. Just as abortion implicates the rights of unborn children who cannot speak up for themselves, the homosexual agenda attacks the rights of young people to a home with both father and mother. Like their counterparts in the abortion movement, homosexuals seek the right to do wrong.

## The Right To Do Wrong

The American judicial system classifies certain rights as fundamental, but homosexuality is not among them—at least not yet. *Fundamental rights* are those "objectively, deeply rooted in this Nation's history and tradition."[21] They're "implicit in the concept of ordered liberty, such that neither liberty nor justice would exist if they were sacrificed."[22] The government must have a very good reason to interfere with a fundamental right. That is why so many abortion restrictions have been struck down. But in spite of the vast expansion of privacy rights, courts have generally been slow to declare a new fundamental right to same-sex intimacy.[23]

Courts hesitate to announce new fundamental rights. Judicial restraint is imperative because newly asserted rights are removed from the arena of public debate and legislative action.[24] The U.S. Supreme Court articulated the absence of a fundamental right to homosexual sodomy in its 1986 *Bowers* decision.[25] Although this case was overruled by *Lawrence* in 2003, *Lawrence* nevertheless declined the invitation to proclaim a new fundamental right.[26] There is ongoing debate about the implications of *Lawrence*, but many courts have agreed that no new fundamental right was announced.[27]

The U.S. Supreme Court (*Romer*) affirmed the Colorado Supreme Court's decision to strike down the state's anti-gay initiative "because it infringed the fundamental right of gays and lesbians to participate in the political process."[28] *Romer* does not rest on any fundamental right to homosexual conduct per se, but rather the simple right to participate in the political process. The Sixth Circuit Court of Appeals reconsidered a case in light of *Romer* and upheld a more carefully drafted anti-gay rights initiative.[29]

Even if there is a sphere of privacy that government may not transgress, and even if some private sexual conduct is deemed a fundamental right, there *should not* be a corollary right to draft unwilling private citizens to assist in the exercise of such rights. But aggressive activists press for the application of anti-discrimination laws to override conscience and compel unwilling accomplices.

The judicial waters are muddied. There is still a little good news—maybe. Federal and state laws have granted protections for health care workers opposed to abortion, but these could soon vanish (Chapter 9). In spite of a multitude of equal protection arguments, homosexuals as a group have not firmly established a right to the special protections granted racial and other similar minorities—until now. Most courts have stopped short of declaring homosexual conduct a fundamental right. But, legal activists continue to argue that homosexuals *should* be granted the same status as racial minorities and that private homosexual intimacy, like abortion, *should* be a fundamental right to privacy. A few courts have agreed. The recently enacted federal *hate crimes legislation*, grants unprecedented special protection to homosexuals that is not enjoyed by other victims of violent crime. Some of the cases favorable to Christians are older, and legal battles continue to rage. Homosexuals and abortionists alike have organized their agendas and launched well-funded nonprofit groups to establish, assert, and defend their newly created legal rights.[30]

Christians must be vigilant. We are called to live in the real world as "salt and light," preaching the gospel and ministering with compassion to others, including homosexuals and women who abort their babies. However, onerous laws preclude believers from legally drawing the line in situations where their faith would be compromised. The spiritual and legal threat cannot be overstated. Homosexuality assaults the male-female distinction ordained by God at creation (Gen. 1:26–27). Biblical condemnation of this sin could not be more emphatic (Lev. 18:22; Rom. 1:26–32). The slaughter of the unborn children attacks the image of God (Gen. 1:26–27; Ps. 139:13–16). Protection of the weak and oppressed is a key component of justice and a recurring theme in Scripture (e.g., Ps. 82:3; Ps. 103:6; Ps. 146:7; Isaiah 1:17; Isa. 10:2; Isa. 58:10; Ezek. 22:7; Dan. 4:27; Amos 2:7; Acts 7:19), and there is hardly a more oppressed person than the unborn child who may never experience life outside the womb. Unless we are alert and act swiftly, believers may soon face persecution in our formerly Christian nation for daring to practice biblical principles in their businesses and professions. The free exercise of religion, guaranteed by the First Amendment, is rapidly being replaced by the *free exercise* of sexual immorality.

# *Eight*

# Jesus Loves the Little Children: Red and Yellow, Black and . . . Gay?

*Or do you not know that the unrighteousness shall not inherit the kingdom of God? Do not be deceived; neither fornicators, nor idolaters, nor adulterers, nor effeminate, nor homosexuals, nor thieves, nor the covetous, nor drunkards, nor revilers, nor swindlers, shall inherit the kingdom of God. And such were some of you; but you were washed, but you were sanctified, and you were justified in the name of the Lord Jesus Christ, and in the Spirit of our God* (1 CORINTHIANS 6:9–11 NASB).

On May 5, 2009, the D.C. Council voted 12–1 to approve legislation providing in relevant part that "[a] marriage legally entered into in another jurisdiction between two persons of the same sex . . . shall be recognized in the District." Mayor Adrian Fenty signed the legislation May 6, 2009 and the bill became law on July 7, 2009.

In early 2007, the Utah Supreme Court reversed a lower court decision granting parental standing to a mother's former partner, a lesbian political activist, who had no legal or biological relationship to the child[1] In 2008, a North Carolina appellate court affirmed a lower court order awarding joint legal custody of a child to two lesbians who had executed a "Parenting Agreement" before they separated.[2] The court claimed to apply a "best interests of the child" standard.

A Virginia woman went through a hysterectomy, double mastectomy, hormone therapy, and name change. In 2002, "he" went to court to obtain an order to force the state Office of Vital Records to correct the gender on "his" birth certificate.[3] If "he" marries a woman, is this a disguised same-sex union? If "he" marries a man in a state that has legalized same-sex "marriage," is that a heterosexual union that Christians should recognize? These bizarre inquiries are no longer fanciful hypotheticals.

Based on the constitutional right to equal protection under the law, homosexuals assert minority status analogous to racial and other groups who have suffered unfair discrimination in past years. That fallacy must be exploded. Unlike race, national origin, gender, or other morally neutral traits that say nothing about a person's conduct or character, homosexuality is inseparably linked to immoral conduct that poses serious health risks. Although Christians preach the gospel of Jesus Christ to all people without discrimination, a politically powerful group defined by a common sin should not be entitled to assert legal rights, under the guise of equal protection and discrimination that erode the religious liberties of other citizens and force them to act against conscience. That is exactly what is happening all over America today.

## Legal Perks and Penalties

Homosexuals have crept into American culture and fostered acceptance of their lifestyle through the media—the 2005 movie "Brokeback Mountain" (two gay cowboys), TV shows like "Will and Grace" and "Queer Eye for the Straight Guy," soap operas, and prime time dramas. But their agenda now demands far more than tolerance. Activists are determined to eradicate their opposition. Their ultimate goal is to marginalize those who discriminate against their lifestyle or hold biblical views of marriage.[4] Homosexuals demand legal perks for themselves while imposing draconian legal and financial penalties on opponents. These penalties arise from a host of laws related to employment, harassment, hate-speech, discrimination, tax exemptions, and family relationships.

In July 2009, homosexual activists celebrated when North Carolina passed the School Violence Prevention Act and the Healthy Youth Act.[5] The anti-bullying bill forces state school districts to adopt policies with special protection for violence motivated by sexual orientation or gender identity. The other measure replaces the state's traditional abstinence-until-marriage teaching with a comprehensive sex education program that opens the door for public school teaching about alternative sexual lifestyles. The National Education Association (NEA), the nation's largest teachers' union, adopted a resolution pledging to support increased rights for same-sex couples. This pledge emerged at the organization's annual meeting, held in San Diego, California, June 29 to July 6, 2009. The only exemption the group acknowledged was the right of religious organizations to refuse to perform or recognize same-sex marriages in violation of their doctrine.[6]

After the Supreme Court affirmed the Boy Scouts' right to exclude homosexuals from their association, other penalties were used to retaliate against their policies. The Scouts have been excluded from a publicly sponsored charitable contribution campaign,[7] evicted from a municipal building they had leased in Philadelphia since 1928,[8] and denied access to a public marina facility in Berkeley, CA.[9]

Tax exemptions can also be used as a powerful lever. In the *Bob Jones University* case, the Supreme Court used exempt status as a lever to compel compliance with the strong public policy in favor of eliminating racial discrimination.[10] Christians can surely affirm racial equality, but the same legal principle could be used as a bludgeon to penalize ministries, even churches, that refuse to abandon the biblical view of homosexuality. A similar potential exists at the state level, where exemptions cover not only income tax but also property and other local taxes. It could become extraordinarily costly to operate a faithful Christian ministry if America ever comes to the point where protection of homosexuality is recognized as strong public policy. Such a result defies the First Amendment guarantees of free speech, religion, and association, but so does the *Bob Jones University* decision.

### One Flesh—One Sex?

Anti-discrimination laws have crept into the legal system across America and now pose one of the greatest threats to religious liberty. Emboldened by these victories, homosexuals now have the audacity to demand legal recognition for same-sex unions, radically redefining marriage and family. The threat to religious freedom will skyrocket. In 2001, the highest state court in New York ruled that Yeshiva University, an institution founded on Orthodox Jewish beliefs, violated state anti-discrimination laws by banning same-sex couples from its *married* dormitory for the Albert Einstein College of Medicine.[11] This is only *one* example, and it arose in a state that had never previously recognized any right to same-sex marriage.

Early American law relied on the God's law to define marriage. The Massachusetts Supreme Court had to distort its own historical record in order to justify its revolutionary decision creating a constitutional right to same-sex marriage: "Simply put, the government creates civil marriage. In Massachusetts, civil marriage is, and since pre-Colonial days has been, precisely what its name implies: a wholly secular institution."[12] But early Massachussetts cases— well beyond pre-Colonial days—looked to Scripture to understand and rule on issues related to marriage. Incestuous marriages were "against the law of God,"[13] obligations of married women were defined with reference to God's law,[14] and state divorce law at one time incorporated the provisions of ecclesiastical law in England.[15] This is hardly the picture of a wholly secular institution.

The challenge to believers is profound. Coerced participation in facilitating the homosexual lifestyle substantially burdens *core* Christian convictions that are entitled to First Amendment protection, whether or not acceptable, logical, consistent, or comprehensible to others. Courts must undertake the often difficult and delicate task of determining what beliefs and practices qualify.[16] Although courts cannot rule as to the truth of religious convictions, some inquiry is indispensable to analyze the nature and extent of the burden to be weighed against competing interests.[17] The dissent in the favorable *Dale* decision sharply criticized the majority's failure to independently analyze how significantly the Boy Scouts' expression was affected by a state's anti-discrimination law.[18] Where core beliefs are implicated, the government has a heavier burden to carry. Even commentators on the opposite side of this issue would leave room for courts to grant an exemption where a *core* religious belief is burdened.[19]

An appropriate theological inquiry would help courts craft satisfactory exemptions yet avoid opening a Pandora's box that would impermissibly entangle them in theology. Christians affirm the Old and New Testaments of the Bible as the eternal, infallible Word breathed out by God. The Bible explains God's creation, the duties human beings owe to Him, and His plan of salvation from sin. *God* ordained the distinction between male and female at creation. He affirmed sexuality as a fundamental element of the created order when He created male and female in His image (Gen. 1:26–27, 2:7, 2:18–23). He ordained their heterosexual union in the covenant of marriage, to bear children and instruct them in His law (Gen. 2:24–25; Deut. 4:9–10). Later, God draws an analogy between husband-wife and Jesus Christ's relationship to His church (Eph. 5:31–32). Homosexual conduct is a grievous perversion of the created order. This sin is not a minor aberration, but a revolutionary attack on God's creation and His plan for both the family and the church. Seminary professor Peter Jones said it well:

> Though presented in the righteous robes of civic justice, homosexuality represents a complete distortion of creation's sexual structures. We cannot understand the radical

implications of homosexuality's acceptance until we realize that homosexuality turns the blueprint for life inside out and upside down.[20]

Sexuality is a basic human distinction that homosexual advocates want to erase. Homosexuality is condemned as an abomination in both the Old and New Testaments (Lev. 18:22; Rom. 1:26–27). Homosexuality is one of three critical exchanges that turns creation on its head in rebellion against God.

- First is the exchange of God's glory for images of created things (Rom. 1:23).
- Second is the exchange of God's truth for a lie, wherein men worship and serve the creature in place of God the Creator (Rom. 1:25).
- Finally, natural heterosexual relations are exchanged for unnatural same-sex relations, "degrading passions" (Rom. 1:26–27). Those who approve such sinful sexual practices are also severely rebuked (Rom. 1:32).

Christian cannot share in the immoral acts of others (Ephesians 5:11). In short, the Christian faith is severely burdened by a legal requirement to actively facilitate an agenda that radically redefines the family relationships God ordained at creation. Erasure of the male-female distinction is tantamount to the pagan monism that blurs the distinction between God the Creator and His creation.

## Apples and Oranges

Sexual orientation discrimination is not analogous to racial or gender discrimination. Homosexuals have never been bought and sold as slaves or denied the right to participate in the political process. There are massive discrepancies between the circumstances of true victims and those manufactured by the gay-rights agenda. Unlike genuine minorities who deserve extra protection to ensure their equality, homosexuals are not a special class entitled to legal perks, and the government has no compelling interest in eliminating discrimination against them. Homosexuals have hijacked legitimate

anti-discrimination laws and added themselves to the list of protected categories.

There is unquestionably an established national policy and
compelling interest in eliminating racial discrimination and segregation. Racial discrimination existed with official approval for
the first one hundred and sixty-five years of American history.[21]
African-Americans were bought and sold as slaves, treated as property rather than persons, and denied even the most elementary civil
rights. Similarly, women were denied the right to vote for many
years, and elimination of gender discrimination has gained increasing recognition as an important state interest.[22]

But homosexual *status* is inseparably linked to homosexual
*conduct*. Comparing homosexuals to racial minorities is a typical
apples-to-oranges scenario. Race and gender are morally neutral
classifications unrelated to conduct. But sexual orientation is inextricably intertwined with the tendency to engage in particular conduct—conduct condemned for centuries as immoral and unhealthy.
The sodomy statutes that homosexuals challenge are laws that
regulate conduct and protect against disease. Courts acknowledge
conduct as an integral component of homosexuality.[23] However,
modern anti-discrimination laws are expanding their reach and
blurring the status-conduct distinction. Some municipal ordinances
include such criteria as prior criminal record or psychiatric treatment, military status, personal appearance, source of income, place
of residence, or political ideology.[24] California has cases covering
families with minor children, age, and association with persons of
unconventional appearance.[25] Some categories are not defined by
reference to conduct, while others are (ex-offenders or psychiatric
patients).

Ironically, homosexuals expect Christians to disengage their
core beliefs from their conduct but are unwilling to do the same.
Activists expect tolerance, accommodation, acceptance, and facilitation of their conduct but would deny believers the right to conduct their lives in conformity to their faith and conscience.

The U.S. Supreme Court rejected an attempt to deny homosexuals basic political protections.[26] Nonetheless, not all discrimination against persons engaged in morally controversial behavior

warrants the same legal penalties as racial or gender discrimination. Race, ethnicity, and gender are morally irrelevant. Homosexuals are defined by conduct that runs contrary to the deeply held moral and religious principles of many Americans. Pedophiles and polygamists are comparable categories. All of these persons already enjoy the same civil rights as everyone else. Moreover, homosexuals do not lack political power. On the contrary, they have successfully organized and lobbied for dramatic changes in the law to advance their agenda.

## Discrimination Defined—or Not

Discrimination becomes legally significant when it's arbitrary, irrational, and unreasonable. However, action—or inaction—consistent with conscience and motivated by deeply held religious convictions is *not* arbitrary, *nor* irrational, and *not* unreasonable. Where discrimination is integrally related to the exercise of a core constitutional right such as religious liberty, it's not the unlawful discrimination rightly targeted by anti-discrimination statutes. A Christian engaged in a business or profession—and seeking faithfully to follow Scripture—would not exclude *all* homosexuals from *all* services. A Christian doctor, for example, would not deny emergency services, surgery, or treatment for disease, but could not in good conscience provide artificial insemination services to facilitate the homosexual redefinition of the family. A Christian lawyer could perform many types of services but could not conscientiously assist a same-sex couple with the adoption of a child or write a legal brief advocating same-sex marriage.

Modern anti-discrimination statutes codify the historic common law duty of a public enterprise to serve all customers on reasonable terms. The original California Unruh Act, for example, originally encompassed "inns, restaurants, hotels, eating-houses, barber-shops, bath-houses, theaters, skating-rinks, and all other places of public accommodation or amusement."[27] The Act gradually expanded to encompass more places and people: a race track could not expel man of immoral character;[28] homosexuals may obtain food and drink at a public restaurant.[29] What the Act clearly forbids is the irrational, arbitrary, or unreasonable discrimination prohibited by the Equal Protection Clause of the Fourteenth Amendment.[30] Discrimination is *arbitrary* where an entire class of persons is excluded without justification.[31] Discrimination is not *arbitrary* where its purpose is to avoid promoting an agenda. In *Hurley,* parade organizers were not required to grant access to a gay organization, but they did not exclude gay individuals from participation in approved marching units.[32] When the Unruh Act amendments were considered in 1974, the California Legislature Counsel cautioned "a construction of the act that would prohibit discrimination on any of the grounds enumerated therein *whether or not such action was arbitrary* would lead to *absurd results.*"[33]

Sexual orientation has been added to the California Unruh Act and similar statutes as an enumerated category. But discrimination is not arbitrary per se when a believer would be required to set aside conscience. A simple meal at the inn could be a wonderful opportunity for evangelism, but in other circumstances, the services requested of a believer may require facilitating a sinful agenda.

Motivation is a critical factor. Although anti-discrimination laws prohibit refusal to conduct business with an entire group based on personal animosity or stereotypes, the First Amendment demands that courts consider religious motivation on a case-by-case basis. In the unemployment cases, the Supreme Court has held that "to consider a religiously motivated resignation to be 'without good cause' tends to exhibit hostility, not neutrality, towards religion."[34] Similarly, a court would exhibit callous disregard for religion by equating religiously motivated conduct with unlawful discrimination. Outwardly, identical acts can have legally opposite results depending on motivation. Killing another person in self-defense is justifiable homicide. The same act, premeditated with malice aforethought, is first degree murder. The former carries no legal penalties, while the latter warrants severe consequences.

Homosexuals insist on protection from discrimination because sexual orientation is a personal characteristic enumerated in statutes like the California Unruh Act, i.e., "traits, conditions, decisions, or choices fundamental to a person's identity, beliefs and self-definition."[35] Religion is also a personal characteristic. Moreover, religion unquestionably falls under the Fourteenth Amendment liberty "to define one's own concept of existence, of meaning, of the universe, and of the mystery of human life."[36] Both parties in a business or professional relationship have protected liberty rights to moral autonomy. When these rights clash, the Christian's right to honor conscience is entitled to no less protection than the homosexual's right to pursue a particular agenda.

## Equal Protection under the Cross

Manasseh was one of the most evil kings to rule over Jerusalem. He rebuilt the high places his father Hezekiah had torn down and set up altars to worship the Baals. He made Asherim and worshipped the host of heaven—the creation instead of the Creator. He even constructed alien altars in the house of the Lord. He practiced witchcraft, divination, and made his sons pass through fire. He consulted mediums and spiritists. He placed the carved image of an idol in the house of God. Scripture tells us that Manasseh's evil deeds exceeded those of the surrounding pagan nations. Finally, the Lord brought the Assyrians against Manassah, and they captured him with hooks, bound him, and took him off to Babylon.[37]

But the story doesn't end there. Miraculously, Manasseh humbled himself greatly before God and cried out to Him. God heard his urgent prayers and returned him to his kingdom in Jerusalem. Then Manasseh knew that the Lord was God.[38]

Believers are faced with urgent legal battles in America today—*spiritual* battles about life, death, marriage, amd family. Aggressive activists work around the clock to silence Christians. They speak of *equal protection under the law*, asserting the right to do what God says is wrong. We wrestle with such people in courtrooms, but at the same time, they're sinners who desperately need God's grace—just as we do.

Righteous anger comes easily amidst the legal battles of our times, but we dare not let it overshadow our mission to bring the glorious good news of the gospel to a sin-infested world. The Apostle Paul declared that Jesus Christ came into the world to save sinners, and that he was among the foremost of these.[39] All have sinned and come short of God's glory.[40] There is equal *protection* under the cross of Christ for all sinners who believe in Him because His precious blood was shed and He satisfied the requirements of God's justice. The Bible holds out hope, *without discrimination*, for homosexuals and all other sinners, through the life, death, and resurrection of Jesus Christ. The apostle Paul reminded the Corinthian Christians that some of them were formerly among those who would not inherit the kingdom of God—including homosexuals—but they had been washed and sanctified in the name of Jesus Christ (1 Cor. 6:9–11). We cannot facilitate the homosexual agenda, but we can interact lovingly with homosexuals and all others entangled in sin, remembering that our own salvation is a free gift of God's grace.

# *Nine*

# The Collision of Law
# and Conscience

*You shall not hate your brother in your heart, but you shall reason frankly with your neighbor, lest you incur sin because of him* (LEVITICUS 19:17 ESV).

As mentioned in Chapter 4, a Christian landlord refused to rent to an unmarried boyfriend-girlfriend because of her religious belief that she would be facilitating sexual sin. The California Supreme Court ruled against her, even though she would have been legally liable for a tenant's use of her property for prostitution.[1] In 2008, the same misguided court ruled against two Christian medical doctors who refused to artificially inseminate a homosexual woman intending to raise a child with her female partner—even though they had referred her to another facility and she gave birth in 2001.[2] A Christian nurse employed by Mount Sinai Hospital in New York was given **no choice** but to facilitate a woman's **choice** to abort her baby.[3]

*S*cripture displays a high regard for human conscience. Christians are instructed to exercise their liberty cautiously so as not to wound the conscience of a weaker believer (1 Cor. 8:1–13, 10:23–33). Nevertheless, in America today, anti-discrimination statutes are on a collision course with conscience and religious liberty. Commentators on both sides observe the legal quagmire:

> When a legislature acts to protect homosexual behavior under antidiscrimination laws, it elevates homosexual practices to the status of protected activities while at the same time branding many mainstream religious institutions and individuals as outlaws engaged in antisocial and immoral behavior.[4]
>
> This conflict between the statutory rights of individuals against private acts of discrimination and the near universally-recognized right of free exercise of religion places a complex legal question involving competing societal values squarely before the courts.[5]

Christians who practice biblical principles in their businesses may face financial ruin or professional displacement if they dare to openly defy antidiscrimination statutes that force them to facilitate politically correct agendas. Doctors, nurses, and pharmacists face similar dilemmas related to abortion and life support. This coercion of personal services violates not only the First Amendment protection for religious liberty, but also the Thirteenth Amendment's prohibition of involuntary servitude. Christians need to be aware of the dangers as well as available legal protections, including state constitutions, statutes, and court decisions that protect us from legal compulsion to act against conscience.

## Commercial Collisions

Conflicts erupt everywhere in the daily world of commerce—housing, employment (Chapter 12), professional licensing and services, school accreditation and training programs, and public accommodations:

- The American College of Obstetricians and Gynecologists refused to accredit a Catholic medical school that would not teach abortion procedures, and a Maryland court upheld their decision.[6]

- Law schools have been unsuccessful in challenging the anti-discrimination accreditation standards of the American Bar Association.[7]
- A marriage counselor who refused to counsel gay couples received no accommodation for her convictions.[8]
- Nurse Toni Lemly was reduced from full-time to part-time employment for her refusal to distribute the morning-after pill. St. Tammany Parish Hospital refused to accommodate her conscientious objections.[9]
- An internet adoption agency based in Arizona abandoned the California market, as part of a settlement agreement, rather than post profiles for same-sex couples wanting to adopt.[10]
- The National Association of Social Workers Code of Ethics, Section IIA–3 provides that: "The social worker should not practice, condone, facilitate or collaborate with any form of discrimination on the basis of race, color, sex, sexual orientation, age, religion, national origin, marital status, political belief, mental or physical handicap, or any other preference or personal characteristic, condition or status."
- The North Carolina Bar Association proposed an amendment to the Rules of Professional Conduct, adding the following statement to the "Preamble: A Lawyer's Responsibilities":

> While employed in a professional capacity, a lawyer should avoid knowingly manifesting through word or deed bias or prejudice based upon a person's race, gender, national origin, religion, age, disability, sexual orientation, marital status, or other protected status or personal characteristic. This does not, however, prohibit legitimate advocacy when such status or personal characteristic is material to the issues in a proceeding.[11]

> (The State Bar Ethics Committee withdrew this controversial amendment after receiving a letter drafted by Alliance Defense Fund and signed by many ADF allied attorneys in North Carolina.)

If the rapidly growing same-sex marriage movement gains momentum, these conflicts will escalate exponentially, impacting county clerks (issuing marriage licenses), judges (performing weddings), and a variety of others services required for weddings:

- After the California Supreme Court manufactured a constitutional "right" to same-sex marriage, San Francisco Mayor Gavin Newsom expressed outrage at San Diego County's decision to allow conscientious clerks to opt out of issuing marriage licenses to same-sex couples.[12]
- Ocean Grove Camp Meeting Association, a United Methodist ministry, declined an application to rent its Boardwalk Pavilion—*a place of worship*—to conduct a same-sex civil-union ceremony in violation of its religious doctrine. Two same-sex couples filed complaints with the New Jersey Division of Civil Rights.[13] The New Jersey Department of Environmental Protection stripped the ministry of its property tax exemption in 2007.[14]
- The New Mexico Human Rights Commission fined a Christian photographer for refusing to take pictures at a same-sex "commitment" ceremony.[15]
- eHarmony.com, a California-based dating service originally publicized through Focus on the Family, expanded its online dating service to include same-sex couples. This nationwide change in policy was one of the terms required to settle a New Jersey lawsuit.[16]

Cases about the free exercise of religion often arise in a commercial context. The state actively regulates many aspects of commerce. Sometimes these regulations conflict with religious faith and a court must determine whether the Constitution mandates an exemption. Believers don't enjoy absolute protection from all government regulation:

> Congress and the courts have been sensitive to the needs flowing from the Free Exercise Clause, but *every* person cannot be shielded from *all* the burdens incident to exercising *every* aspect of the right to practice religious beliefs. When

followers of a particular sect enter into commercial activity as a matter of choice, the limits they accept on their own conduct as a matter of conscience and faith are not to be superimposed on the statutory schemes which are binding on others in that activity.[17]

But Christians don't forfeit their constitutional rights when they enter the commercial sphere—no one does. Religious freedom is more limited in the business world but not abrogated altogether. Religion does not end where daily business begins. Its moral precepts cannot be relegated to the private fringes of life. If believers were required to abandon their moral principles they would be squeezed out of full participation in civic life and the liberties of the First Amendment would ring hollow.[18]

## Conscience Clauses: Taking Up the Shield of Faith in the Courtroom

It should not be a crime to follow conscience. Respect for individual conscience is deeply rooted in our nation's history. For example, the moral dilemma created by mandatory military service has long been recognized through statutory and judicially crafted exemptions. One such case, recognizing man's "duty to a moral power higher than the State," quotes Harlan Fiske Stone (who later served as Chief Justice):

> ... both morals and sound policy require that the state should not violate the conscience of the individual. All our history gives confirmation to the view that liberty of conscience has a moral and social value which makes it worthy of preservation at the hands of the state. So deep in its significance and vital, indeed, is it to the integrity of man's moral and spiritual nature that nothing short of the self-preservation of the state should warrant its violation; and it may well be questioned whether the state which preserves its life by a settled policy of violation of the conscience of the individual will not in fact ultimately lose it by the process." Stone, *The Conscientious Objector*, 21 Col. Univ. Q. 253, 269 (1919).[19]

Following *Roe v. Wade*, Congress has acted several times to protect health care workers and institutions from coerced participation in abortion. The Church Amendment[20] prohibits using federal funds as a lever to force an institution or individual to perform abortion or sterilization procedures contrary to conscience. The Danforth Amendment to the Civil Rights Restoration Act of 1987[21] expands on the "Church Amendment" by prohibiting discrimination against health care providers that refuse to be associated with abortions. Health training programs, doctors, and medical students cannot be denied otherwise available federal funding because they refuse to participate in abortion. The Hyde-Weldon Conscience Protection Amendment, passed in 2004, denies funding to governmental entities and agencies that discriminate against health care entities or workers that don't provide or participate in abortion.

Most states have enacted statutory conscience clauses.[22] Some are under-inclusive and will not cover a particular situation, because legislators cannot pinpoint the myriad of circumstances where a law might jeopardize religious freedom. However, considerable case law reflects a high respect for conscience, particularly in the health care industry.

Patients and doctors both have legal rights to moral autonomy. However, "to demand of a physician that he or she act in a manner she deems to be morally unpalatable not only compromises the physician's ethical integrity, but is also likely to have a corrosive effect upon the dedication and zeal with which she ministers to patients."[23] Eradicating the doctor's rights erodes the quality of medical care, and courts consistently uphold conscience rights.[24] The hospital or doctor may be required to cooperate in moving a patient.[25] Hospital ethics are also respected, but one court overruled a hospital policy because management had not consulted or considered the views of the individual treating physicians.[26] Prior notice to patients may also be important. One facility lost in court because its policy was not disclosed to the patient's family until they attempted to withdraw artificial nutrition and hydration,[27] but a patient who is properly notified might waive the right to object if a conflict later arises.

Some state constitutions grant more protection than the U.S. Constitution. The California Constitution describes religious freedom as "liberty of conscience" to be infringed only where conduct is "licentious or inconsistent with the peace or safety of the State."[28] California's constitution also provides that no person shall be "disqualified from entering or pursuing a business, profession . . . because of . . . creed . . ."[29] Other states with similar constitutional language have held that justice demanded analysis under the state constitution so as to avoid *Smith's* restriction of religious liberty.[30]

Constitutions typically limit religious liberty if it interferes with public peace or safety. No one would seriously argue that Islamic extremists have the right to hijack airplanes and murder thousands of Americans because their religion demands it. Courts deny religious exemptions where accommodation would endanger minor children and/or community health.[31] In such cases, religious conduct "invariably pose[s] some substantial threat to public safety, peace or order."[32] Sometimes modern activists point to historic events like the Crusades, Inquisition, and Salem witch trials to argue against accommodating religion.[33] But peacefully declining business poses no true danger to others. Conscientious objection claims rarely endanger the community and are "very close to the core of religious liberty."[34]

The peace-safety provisos are evidence that protection extends to both conduct and convictions. This language would be superfluous if religious liberty applied solely to beliefs. Some religious practices may be abhorrent to some yet constitutionally protected.[35] Free exercise is not limited to outright prohibitions of religious practice, nor should it be understood as an unrestrained right of personal autonomy that precludes reasonable regulations for public health and safety.[36]

However, if a state constitution protects an illegitimate right like abortion, it may trump statutory protections for conscientious objectors. An Alaska hospital prohibited abortions unless necessary to save the mother's life or in cases of incest. Its policy was held unconstitutional—contrary to their reproductive freedom guaranteed by the state constitution—in spite of state conscience protection, because the hospital was a quasi-public institution and not affiliated with any religion.[37]

## Liberty and Justice for Some

Antidiscrimination laws provide liberty and justice for politically powerful minorities while denying it altogether for those compelled to serve their agenda. There are many predictable situations where believers—like the Christian physicians in *Benitez*—may be required to perform personal services that actively facilitate a morally objectionable agenda. In recent news, there are blatant attacks on existing conscience clauses that protect health care professionals from participating in abortions. In late 2008, Senators Hillary Clinton (D-N.Y.) and Patty Murray (D-Wash.) introduced legislation to restrain implementation of a conscience protection rule enacted by the U.S. Department of Health and Human Services (HHS).[38] In January 2009, the ACLU, representing the National Family Planning & Reproductive Health Association, filed a federal lawsuit in Connecticut to halt enforcement of the new HHS conscience protection regulations.[39] This is untenable in a country dedicated to liberty and justice for *all*.

The Thirteenth Amendment to the U.S. Constitution, ratified in 1865, was intended to abolish slavery and involuntary servitude:

> Section 1. Neither slavery nor involuntary servitude, except as a punishment for crime whereof the party shall have been duly convicted, shall exist within the United States, or any place subject to their jurisdiction.
>
> Section 2. Congress shall have power to enforce this article by appropriate legislation. This Amendment is violated when an individual has "no available choice but to work or be subject to legal sanction."[40] Courts decline to specifically enforce personal service contracts because enforcement might constitute involuntary servitude.[41] Significant friction and social costs are implicated in forcing estranged parties to reunite, particularly where the services require mutual confidence.

In some situations, enforcing anti-discrimination laws would not require an individual to perform personal services that violate religious convictions or directly facilitate a controversial agenda—restaurant service or country club membership rights, for example.[42] But requiring a *particular* physician to fertilize a lesbian, requiring a *particular* nurse to facilitate an abortion, or requiring a *particular* attorney to assist a same-sex couple's adoption, compels the performance of services that actively facilitate an objectionable agenda. Such services are qualitatively different from selling a product or providing the less personal services associated with access to a public restaurant, hotel, or club.

This involuntary servitude argument would only apply to individuals, not entities. It would have limited usefulness for a business employing various individuals, a medical clinic, a pharmacy, a law firm—or even a religious ministry. In one California antidiscrimination case against a medical clinic, the court highlighted the defendant's *corporate* status in rejecting a personal services argument.[43] The complaint did not seek to compel any individual physician to form or continue a doctor-patient relationship. The clinic could comply with the law without the court ordering the services of a specific doctor. Meanwhile, the employing entity might be able—or even legally required—to accommodate an individual employee's religious convictions.

These observations about the Thirteenth Amendment are important for free exercise claims by individuals required to act against conscience. The watershed 1990 *Smith* decision suggests that courts should apply strict scrutiny where a religious freedom claim is accompanied by the violation of another independent constitutional right. An involuntary servitude claim could fill in this gap.

## Broadly Tailored to Achieve a Political Purpose

When law substantially infringes a core constitutional right, it should be narrowly tailored to accomplish a compelling government purpose.

A statute is narrowly tailored if it targets and eliminates no more than the exact source of the evil it seeks to remedy. . . . A complete ban can be narrowly tailored, but only if each activity within the proscription's scope is an appropriately targeted evil.[44] But many legal protections for immorality are broadly tailored to achieve a politically correct purpose—eliminating any inconvenience that impedes access to abortion or dignity harms to those who practice sexual perversions. Abortion rights activists want to eradicate even minimal obstructions. Homosexuals seek a complete ban on all sexual orientation discrimination. If a necessary, service is involved, such as emergency room medical treatment, that argument is persuasive. Sexual orientation is truly irrelevant, but activists want much more, running roughshod over religious liberty and framing their demands in the broadest possible terms.

This is a *moral* battle. The government should not impose a particular view of sexual morality on religious institutions and individuals who operate their ministries and businesses according to religious convictions.[45] Yet some accuse the *Christian right* of attempting to codify the biblical view that homosexual conduct is sinful.[46] Can these conflicting legal rights be reconciled and protected? Must the state protect *either* homosexuals against discrimination *or* the free exercise of Christianity? Does protection of homosexuals mandate compelling believers to act against their deepest convictions when operating a business, at the risk of financial ruin or professional displacement? Courts often walk a tightrope in their obligation to protect all citizens, not just a minority screaming discrimination.

The First Amendment protects against government coercion to endorse or subsidize a cause.[47] The government has no power to force a *speaker* to either support or oppose a particular viewpoint.[48] Thus the state may not coerce approval of homosexual conduct.[49] But the legal analysis is more complex when something beyond pure speech is involved.

The *Dale* dissent suggested that compliance with antidiscrimination statutes would not force an organization "to take any position on the legitimacy of any individual's private beliefs or private conduct."[50] The *Benitez* plaintiff argued that the doctors' refusal to inseminate her was not a vehicle for conveying a message.[51] Conduct does not necessarily express a position. Providing emergency care or treatment for disease implies nothing about the morality of a patient's conduct. But *Benitez* involved facilitating the pregnancy of a lesbian woman intending to raise a child with her female partner. The doctor was required to actively perform services that promote a radical redefinition of the family, becoming a de facto accomplice to a morally objectionable agenda. Homosexuals may have a legal right to same-sex adoption, just as pregnant women have the legal right to abortion, but in neither case is there an accompanying right to draft an unwilling accomplice. In this clash of autonomies, other persons should have a right to choose not to participate.[52] State coercion of personal services compromises both personal and professional integrity, particularly in a relationship where fiduciary obligations are not easily divorced from moral convictions.

A state mandate to engage in sinful conduct is essentially a statement that "no religious believers who refuse to do X [sinful act] may be included in this part of our social life."[53] Banning religious believers from participation in society is contrary to the First Amendment and our American traditions. Religious liberty is decimated when secular ideologies employ the strong arm of the state to advance their causes, promoting tolerance and respect for some (homosexuals) while ruthlessly suppressing others (Christians).[54] Courts urgently need to protect religious citizens from coerced promotion of an agenda they cannot support.

The strict scrutiny needed to limit a fundamental right normally requires a compelling government interest. In the past, commentators speculated that even a well-drafted antidiscrimination statute would not withstand a free exercise challenge.[55] There is no firm national policy comparable to other categories entitled to heightened protection.[56]

Some courts speak of a compelling interest in eliminating *all* invidious discrimination.[57] Such broad language requires analysis of the particular act of discrimination and careful balancing of the interests at stake. Even where a compelling interest exists, courts have required the government to show a compelling interest in *not* granting an exemption, and it's feasible to conduct case-by-case evaluations.[58] Amish parents are entitled to exempt their children from compulsory high school education.[59] But it would be unduly burdensome to accommodate the Amish by granting broad exemptions from Social Security taxes.[60]

It is instructive to consider anti-gay-rights initiatives that have survived judicial scrutiny after the Colorado measure failed in *Romer*.[61] These are valid reasons to enact laws ensuring that anti-discrimination laws are not applied in a manner that encroaches the basic rights of others. Such purposes include the "augmentation of individual autonomy imbedded in personal conscience and morality" and protection of voters against legal compulsion "to expend their own public and private resources to guarantee and enforce nondiscrimination against gays in local commercial transactions and social intercourse."[62]

It is difficult to imagine a compelling interest in not granting a carefully defined exemption to a Christian who cannot subscribe to a morally controversial political agenda. But although past court decisions have rarely found any compelling interest in eliminating sexual orientation discrimination, the scene could be rapidly changing.[63] The D.C. Court of Appeals found such an interest two decades ago when it compelled a religious university to recognize a homosexual student group.[64] Recent state court decisions in Connecticut,[65] Iowa,[66] and California[67] have based the right to same-sex marriage on what the courts imagine to be a compelling interest in eliminating discrimination against homosexuals. The Massachusetts same-sex marriage decision in 2003 could not even find a *rational*—let alone *compelling*—interest in limiting marriage to opposite-sex couples.[68] The law has taken an ominous direction that merits our attention, concern, and action.

## Bright and Blurry Lines

Jesus laid down His rights and took the form of a servant, humbling Himself and suffering in silence in order to go to the cross (Phil. 2:6–8; 1 Pet. 2:22–24). We are often called to follow His example and not aggressively assert our rights (Phil. 2:5ff; 1 Pet. 2:21ff). But if the civil law mandates sin, we must obey God instead. That could mean claiming a constitutional right, possibly setting precedent that will help other believers. How can Christians know when their conduct is actively facilitating sin? How remote is too remote?

- A believer sells bedroom furniture. A bed can be used for a married couple or a single person—or for prostitution, adultery, incest, molestation, or homosexual intimacy.
- A believer owns a restaurant that provides catering for special events. Serving a meal to a homosexual does not actively facilitate sin—Jesus shocked the religious leaders when He ate with all sorts of sinners—but what about serving the food for a same-sex "wedding" ceremony?

There are a myriad of possible scenarios requiring prayer and careful application of Scripture to draw the right lines. Believers must guard against participating in the sins of others, but withdrawal from the world truncates the Great Commission. Our testimony and attitude are important in showing the world what it means to follow Christ (Matt. 5:16).

A few court cases provide insight about where a court might draw the line. Years ago, a Jehovah's Witness successfully asserted the right to quit his job and collect unemployment, because he objected to his employer's manufacturing of turrets for military tanks.[69] This precedent provides breathing room for conscientious objections. The job did not require active participation in battle, but Mr. Thomas objected to indirectly promoting war through the manufacturing operation. The Supreme Court did not consider that conduct too remote to qualify for a religious exemption. Two antidiscrimination cases in Minnesota illustrate judicial line drawing. A deli owner's refusal to deliver food to an abortion clinic was not unlawful discrimination, because he opposed their practice of performing abortions.[70] However, a health club owner's refusal to admit homosexual members conflicted with his own statements that he opposed homosexual conduct yet cared for homosexuals as people.[71] Club admission did not signify approval of homosexual acts or facilitate such conduct—and it could have opened the door for evangelism and ministry.

Many people argue that the interests of both parties are best served through referral to another source that can provide the objectionable service.[72] Some would nevertheless find the violation of a protected dignity interest, for example, where a same-sex couple must endure the humiliation of another person objecting to their union. Even where referrals are a permitted accommodation, conscience may only be protected if there is another person available to perform the service and there is no substantial inconvenience to the party seeking services. Moreover, having to provide a referral can be objectionable because it indirectly facilitates the sin. From a legal perspective, referral is a better alternate than coerced facilitation of sin, but it's not a perfect solution.

## The Rising Price of Faith

Jesus Christ shed His own precious blood, sacrificing His life to redeem us from our sins. There is no higher price. American Christians have enjoyed great freedom to preach the gospel and practice their faith, but the scene is changing and the price is rising.

What will it cost American Christians to follow God's law when it locks horns with state mandates and the conflict cannot be avoided? Court cases over the years illustrate the types of burdens believers may face:

*1. Condition for government benefit:* Christians might be forced to choose between following their faith and receiving a government benefit, such as unemployment benefits,[73] tax-exempt status for a ministry,[74] welfare benefits,[75] a driver's license,[76] or official recognition for a student group. [77] This type of burden is of a "wholly different, less intrusive nature than affirmative compulsion or prohibition, by threat of penal sanctions, for conduct that has religious implications."[78] It's "far removed from the historical instances of religious persecution and intolerance that gave concern to those who drafted the Free Exercise Clause of the First Amendment."[79] Nevertheless, legally cognizable harm is caused by compelling a person to choose between adherence to conscience and an important benefit.[80]

**2. Financial sacrifice or inconvenience (without discontinuing the activity):** A statute that coerces a believer, by imposing the risk of substantial penalties if he follows his faith, imposes a burden far greater than a law which incidentally makes religious practice more difficult.[81] In order to comply with their faith, religious citizens have been compelled to observe Sunday closing laws,[82] forego exempt status with the IRS,[83] comply with recordkeeping, minimum wage, and overtime pay requirements,[84] pay the employer's share of Social Security tax,[85] grant tangible benefits (but not endorsement) to a student gay rights group,[86] and discontinue employee health insurance.[87] In each of these cases, believers could continue the activity at issue while observing religious commands.

**3. Criminal penalties for religiously required conduct:** It's hard to imagine that compliance with the Christian faith would ever result in criminal charges, but it could happen someday. Criminal laws have interfered with religious beliefs concerning Mormon polygamy,[88] Jehovah's Witness child evangelists,[89] Amish parents' right to educate their children,[90] and Native American ceremonial use of illegal drugs.[91] As America wanders further from its Christian roots, believers should be alert to the threat that future criminal laws might conflict with their faith. This is a real possibility with the pending federal hate crimes legislation.

**4. Discontinue the activity altogether or violate conscience/ religion:** Case results vary, but discontinuing an activity altogether is far more oppressive than continuing to conduct it at greater expense or inconvenience.[92] If antidiscrimination laws are broadly applied, persons who believe homosexuality is sinful are faced with the gruesome choice to either violate their religious convictions and sin under the state's compulsion, or get out of business.[93] Christian landlords have already suffered at the hands of unsympathetic courts who suggest they get out of the rental business if renting to particular persons conflicts with their faith.[94]

The burden on a doctor, lawyer, or other professional is remarkably similar to the *Sherbert* claimant in its impact on their livelihood.[95] Actually, it's far *more* onerous because it potentially forces them out of business, rather than forfeiting temporary benefits.

Advancing the homosexual agenda or facilitating abortion impacts the central tenets of Christianity.[96] The severity of the burden escalates where the law compels a believer to act contrary to fundamental teachings of his religion. One commentator wisely suggests that avoidance of sin (religious forbidden behavior) be considered "per se integral to religious practice," entitling believers to strict scrutiny.[97]

As we saw in Chapter 3, the Supreme Court has weakened protection for religious liberty where an allegedly neutral law of general applicability conflicts with faith. But a law that reflects only one side of a morally controversial issue is hardly neutral.[98] Moreover, a law may satisfy formal neutrality yet lack substantive neutrality where it encourages or discourages religious practice.[99] Even pro-homosexual commentators acknowledge that viewing homosexuality as immoral cannot be divorced from religion.[100] It's inadequate to consider an anti-discrimination law neutral merely because it does not openly target religiously motivated discrimination. The operation of a law appearing neutral on its face may give rise to an inference that religious beliefs actually are targeted.[101] The Massachusetts statute at issue in *Hurley* did not appear to target speech or to discriminate based on content, and parade organizers did not exclude individual homosexuals from participating in their St. Patrick's Day parade, but the antidiscrimination law was applied in a way that violated their First Amendment rights to free association. Similarly, it violates the Free Exercise Clause to apply antidiscrimination laws in a manner that compels Christians to act against conscience in conducting their businesses and ministries. The price to practice our faith is rapidly rising.

# Part Three

# Religious Wrongs: Shoving Christians in the Closet

You are the light of the world. A city set on a hill cannot be hidden. . . . In the same way, let your light shine before others so that they may see your good works and give glory to your Father who is in heaven (Matthew 5:14, 16 ESV).

Gideon members were threatened with arrest for distributing Bibles on a public bike path/sidewalk near a public school in Florida.* A federal court held that the state's School Safety Zone Statute was too vague to enforce.

While activists are busy creating new civil rights, religious wrongs are being perpetrated on Christians who attempt to practice biblical principles and share their faith. Believers don't forfeit their First Amendment rights when they step outside the church. Using the misunderstood phrase "separation of

---

*Gray v. Kohl* (S.D. Fla. 2008) 568 F.Supp.2d 1378.

church and state," some court decisions excise religious expression from the public square, shoving Christians into a closet like the one from which homosexuals have recently emerged. There are a few encouraging notes in recent Supreme Court rulings about public religious displays. However, believers increasingly encounter legal obstacles to being the salt and light of the earth.

# *Ten*

# Purging the
# Public Square

*Where there is no revelation, the people cast off restraint, but
blessed is he who keeps the law* (PROVERBS 29:18 NIV).

In Hendersonville, North Carolina, the Transylvania Board of Commissioners unanimously voted to preserve its tradition of opening board meetings with prayer. They were encouraged by some 1,500 concerned citizens in this courageous decision, after receiving threats from the ACLU in April 2007.[1] In Montana, members of the Bozeman Senior Center successfully reinstated the singing of a traditional Christian doxology before their meals, after similar ACLU threats.[2]

*A*ctivist groups are on a rampage, aggressively utilizing court precedents to remove religious expression from public life. Lawsuits are filed and threatening letters written to excise prayer from city councils and public school events. Religious displays on public property are often challenged, including nativity scenes, war memorials, and Ten Commandments monuments. The phrase "under God" in our Pledge of Allegiance has been attacked, and even our National Motto, "In God We Trust," that appears on our coins has been assailed. The religious history of America is being erased before our very eyes.

## No Sabbath Rest for the Courts

The erosion of America's religious heritage can be seen in some of the cases related to state Sunday Blue Laws, requiring commercial business to shut down on Sundays. In 1961, the Supreme Court upheld the convictions of seven department store employees who sold goods on Sunday in violation of state law. There was a rational secular reason to give all citizens a common day of rest, so the law did not violate the Establishment Clause even though it coincided with the religious beliefs of many Christians.[3] The same year the Court turned a deaf ear to Jewish merchants who complained of having to close their shops on Saturday (their Sabbath) *and* on Sunday. The court refused to exempt them from the closing law, in spite of the inconvenience and loss of revenue.[4] But by 1985, the tide had turned. Connecticut had repealed its Sunday closing laws but prohibited an employer from dismissing an employee who refused to work on his Sabbath. A retail store manager invoked that law when his employer began requiring him to work some Sundays, but he was dismissed. Rather than finding the law a reasonable accommodation for religious employees, the Supreme Court struck it down as a violation of the Establishment Clause.[5] The Court thus drifted from upholding laws honoring the Sabbath to striking down a statute that protected employees wanting to observe it.

## The Lord and the Legislature

The Nebraska legislature had made it a practice for over a century to open sessions with a brief word of prayer, offered by a chaplain paid with state funds. For sixteen years, a Presbyterian minister had performed this service and received a monthly salary. But one disgruntled legislator sued, claiming an Establishment Clause violation because the minister was paid with public funds.[6] The

Supreme Court noted the long American tradition of opening legislative sessions with prayer—a tradition that coexisted with disestablishment and religious freedom. The first Congress appointed and paid a chaplain for each house—then drafted the First Amendment. It's difficult to believe these early congressmen would forbid a practice that they had just engaged in. The long-standing practice of legislative prayer merely acknowledges that Americans are a religious people, reflecting widely held beliefs but not attempting to proselytize or place an official seal of approval on a particular religious belief or practice.

This is good precedent, but the story does not end there. Attacks on legislative prayer continue, particularly where a Christian offers prayer in the name of Jesus Christ. There are many local challenges like the one in Transylvania County, often initiated by groups like the ACLU, Americans United for Separation of Church and State, American Atheists, and Freedom From Religion Foundation. In 2007, Alliance Defense Fund distributed informational letters and launched an educational web page[7] to assist local governments and citizens by providing information about the law and offering free legal assistance, including drafting model prayer policies and defending litigation. The battle is not over[8] but there is an army in place and a growing arsenal of ammunition.

## Bah Humbug

What could be more normal in December than a Christmas tree or nativity scene in the public square? Again, aggressive non-believers cry, "bah humbug!" and take their complaints to the courts. Christmas displays on public property have sparked lawsuits and courts have split hairs to resolve them. A few such cases have gone all the way to the Supreme Court, with mixed results.

In 1984, the Supreme Court ruled on a lawsuit the ACLU filed against the City of Pawtuckett, Rhode Island because its annual Christmas display included a nativity scene, along with Santa's reindeer, a Christmas tree, candy-striped poles, carolers, and other traditional decorations. The crèche included figurines of baby Jesus, Mary and Joseph, angels, shepherds, kings, and animals. It had been part of the display for over forty years before the ACLU challenged it. The annual display sat in the heart of the shopping district on land owned by a nonprofit organization. The Court wisely concluded that the display was not a government establishment of religion. Any benefit to one faith was indirect, remote, and incidental—not sufficient to violate the Constitution.[9]

The ACLU did not give up. Four years later, they were back in the Supreme Court, this time arguing that Allegheny County impermissibly endorsed religion by including both a creche *and* an 18-foot Chanukah menorah in its holiday display at the courthouse in downtown Pittsburgh. The Holy Name Society donated the crèche, which included a banner proclaiming "Gloria in Excelsis Deo" (Glory to God in the Highest). A Jewish group, Chabad, owned the menorah but the city stored, erected, and removed it each year. The Court held the crèche unconstitutional because it promoted Christian praise to God, but found the menorah merely a visual holiday symbol with a secular dimension—thus constitutional.[10]

A few years later, the Court ruled in favor of the Ku Klux Klan after they were denied the opportunity to place a cross on the statehouse plaza in Columbus, Ohio during the 1993 Christmas season. Ohio law had opened Capitol Square to the public for discussions and other public activities. The proposed cross was not a statement by the government about religion, but a *private* statement protected by the First Amendment.[11]

The Christmas controversy did not end with these cases. Confusion and attacks have multiplied in schools and other public venues across the country. In October 2003, Alliance Defense Fund announced its launching of an annual nationwide Christmas Project to defend Christmas expressions and combat censorship.[12] Some of that censorship has risen to high levels of absurdity, as in the case of a young public school child who was told he could not distribute candy-cane ornaments to his friends, with cards explaining the history of the holiday treat, because of the so-called "separation of church and state."[13]

The Christmas cases are legion, but Christmas is only one of many religious expressions that activists try to purge from the public square.

## A Walk in the Park

If you take a walk in Pleasant Grove City's Pioneer Park, you will be pleasantly surprised to see a monument of the Ten Commandments. But local officials in this Utah community had to make a trip to the Supreme Court to keep it there.

Pleasant Grove City has an area set aside in Pioneer Park to commemorate its pioneer history. City officials accept donations of monuments related to that history or given by a civic group with strong ties to the community. The Fraternal Order of Eagles donated a monument of the Ten Commandments to the city in 1971. But years later, the City was sued by Summum, a religious group demanding the right to erect a monument of its "Seven Aphorisms" in Pioneer Park. The Tenth Circuit Court of Appeals ruled in Summum's favor, which the U.S. Supreme Court unanimously reversed.[14]

The city's display was comparable to a museum or public library—not a public forum where all speakers must be allowed and government cannot discriminate on the basis of viewpoint. Although the government may not speak to promote or endorse a particular religious viewpoint, passive displays may acknowledge America's rich religious heritage without transgressing the Establishment Clause: "The fact that government buildings continue to preserve artifacts of [the country's religious] history does not mean that they necessarily support or endorse the particular messages contained in those artifacts."[15]

Under remarkably similar facts, the Supreme Court in 2005, upheld the display of a Ten Commandments monument on the grounds of the Texas state capitol, a twenty-two-acre area containing seventeen monuments and twenty-one historical markers described by a state legislative resolution as commemorating the "people, ideals, and events that compose Texan identity."[16] The Decalogue has religious significance but has also played a significant role in America's heritage that governments may acknowledge through a passive display on public property.[17]

Government may display art with religious content in an exhibit or museum. A university's exhibition of a statue titled

"Holier Than Thou" was offensive to the Catholic plaintiffs who sued to have it removed but did not violate the Establishment Clause. The university exercised editorial discretion in the selection of artwork and had no improper religious motivation.[18] In the same way, the Supreme Court agreed that Pleasant Grove City could display historically relevant items that acknowledge the role of religion in its local history.

Battles over the Ten Commandments extend far beyond the park, and results in other contexts have been much more discouraging. It's disheartening to see the Court's removal of the Commandments from public school classrooms because students might actually read and obey them:

> If the posted copies of the Ten Commandments are to have any effect at all, it will be to induce the schoolchildren to read, meditate upon, perhaps to venerate and obey, the Commandments. However desirable this might be as a matter of private devotion, it's not a permissible state objective under the Establishment Clause.[19]

Beyond the classroom, the Ten Commandments have been banned from the courtroom. The ACLU successfully challenged a Decalogue display posted in two Kentucky county courthouses, even though each was part of a larger Foundations of American Law and Government exhibit. The state legislature had acknowledged Christ as the Prince of Ethics, but the Supreme Court found no secular purpose for the display—only an impermissible religious one.[20] This unfortunate decision came down the same year as the favorable *Van Orden* ruling that allowed the Ten Commandments to stand on the Texas state capitol grounds.

Even more shocking is the treatment of Judge Roy Moore, former Chief Justice of the Alabama Supreme Court. Alabama's nine-member judicial ethics panel unanimously voted to remove him from office in 2003 for his refusal to remove the Ten Commandments from the state judicial building rotunda.[21] This disgraceful action was taken after a federal judge ordered Moore to remove the monument[22] because it violated the Establishment Clause.[23] This courageous former judge—who chose to sacrifice his position rather than dishonor God—has now formed the Foundation for Moral Law, a nonprofit, tax-exempt organization in Montgomery, Alabama, to continue the battle for religious freedom through education and litigation.[24]

In a more remote park setting, a former employee of the National Park Service (NPS) sued to challenge yet another type of semi-religious display: a cross-shaped war memorial, honoring World War I veterans, in the middle of the Mohave Desert Preserve.[25] The plaintiff is a Roman Catholic who does not personally object to the cross, but filed the lawsuit only because another NPS employee was denied permission to erect a Buddhist shrine on the same property. The Ninth Circuit Court of Appeals found a violation of the Establishment Clause even after Congress enacted legislation to authorize the government's fair market value sale of the land to Veterans of Foreign Wars, a private organization.[26] This case now awaits a decision by the U.S. Supreme Court.[27] It has implications for similar war memorials on public property across the country. Even Arlington Cemetery is at risk. It would be tragic to dishonor the soldiers who have bled and died for this country to have to bulldoze the many memorials established to remember them, merely because of a lone heckler's veto.

## In *God* We Trust

Michael Newdow, atheist, self-proclaimed "minister," and founder of the First Amendment Church of True Science ("FACTS"), sued Congress in late 2005 because he objected to the National Motto displayed on American currency: IN GOD WE TRUST. The federal district court, and even the often-liberal Ninth Circuit Court of Appeals, rightly kicked this case out of court. The motto is not a government attempt to evangelize or coerce religious faith.[28] Ironically, Newdow's right to speak freely about his atheism is one of those inalienable rights given by our *Creator*—the God that Newdow rejects—according to America's Declaration of Independence.

Newdow has been active in the courts to erase our religious heritage from public view. Prior to his challenge to the National

Motto, he filed a lawsuit on behalf of his school-age daughter—who does not share his atheism—objecting to the phrase "under God" in our Pledge of Allegiance.[29] The Supreme Court kicked out the case because Newdow did not have custody of his daughter, but commented that: "It would be ironic indeed if this Court were to wield our constitutional commitment to religious freedom so as to sever our ties to the traditions developed to honor it."[30]

Ironic indeed. The Establishment Clause does not require that the public square be purged of all religious symbolism. The Religion Clauses work together to protect religious freedom from government interference. But activists continue their quest to purge the public square and the war is not likely to end soon.

Eleven

# Penetrating the
# Public Schools

*And these words that I am command you today shall be on your heart. You shall teach them diligently to your children, and shall talk of them when you sit in your house, and when you walk by the way, and when you lie down, and when you rise* (Deuteronomy 6:6–7 ESV).

A ten-year-old elementary student In Tennessee was ordered to stop reading his Bible with friends during recess and to stop bringing his Bible to school.[1] A first grader in Los Angeles, California was forbidden to share a Christmas song during "show and tell."[2] A New Jersey elementary student was denied permission to sing "Awesome God" at a school talent show.[3] School district officials in Missouri prohibited teachers from participating in "See You at the Pole" to pray for their schools on their own time.[4] School officials in Raleigh, North Carolina made plans to show teens a sexually explicit film, "American History X," without parental notice or consent.[5] All of these incidents were successfully resolved by Alliance Defense Fund attorneys, but similar scenarios are played out across America with alarming frequency and sometimes litigation is required.

*T*he American public school system has been fertile ground for religion cases over the past half century. Here is where many impressionable young people spend most of their waking hours, often returning after class for extracurricular events and activities. The experience normally culminates with a high school graduation ceremony. During the first eighteen years of life, most young Americans are immersed in the public school system, absorbing its values and ideals. The presence or absence of religion in this environment may have profound, life-long consequences.

What began as a commitment to religious neutrality, intended to ensure liberty to American citizens, has degenerated into a thinly veiled judicial hostility toward public religious expression. Liberal activists have invaded the public schools to remove biblical truth and indoctrinate our children. Courts have expelled prayer, Bible reading, and even moments of silence. Homosexuals can enjoy their "Day of Silence" but Christian students who peacefully participate in a "Day of Truth" risk suspension. Parents must be vigilant because they're often not notified of school officials' plans to indoctrinate their children with immoral views of sexuality or promoting a daughter's "choice" to abort her unborn child.

**Don't You Dare . . . Say a Prayer**
*Reading, writing, count to ten*
*Learn your A B C ' s and then*
*Play outside in open air*
*But don't you dare . . . say a prayer*
*Learn to use a condom well*
*You'll never hear of heaven or hell*
*Speak your mind, curse or swear*
*But don't you dare . . . say a prayer*
*Evolution taught as science*
*Gays can have their "Day of Silence"*
*Speak God's truth—you're out of there*
*'cause you don't dare . . . say a prayer*
**Pray without ceasing** (1 Thessalonians 5:17 ESV).

Both before and after the Supreme Court created the infamous *Lemon* test, the modern wall of separation has been used to banish religious expression from public school classrooms. Prayer was excised in 1962,[6] the year before the Supreme Court banned Bible reading. The Board of Education in New Hyde Park, New York, required the following prayer to be said out loud at the beginning of each school day in every classroom in the school district:

> "Almighty God, we acknowledge our dependence upon Thee, and we beg Thy blessings upon us, our parents, our teachers and our Country."[7]

The parents of ten schoolchildren challenged this simple prayer and the Supreme Court agreed that it violated the First Amendment. The Court explained that:

> It is a matter of history that this very practice of establishing governmentally composed prayers for religious services was one of the reasons which caused many of our early colonists to leave England and seek religious freedom in America.[8]

The state court had found the prayer constitutional so long as no student was compelled to join in it over his own or his parents' objections.[9] Breaking with established American tradition, the Supreme Court ruled it unconstitutional to use the public school system to merely *encourage* children to recite a short prayer.[10] Dissenting Justice Stewart highlights the religious heritage the majority overlooked:

> One of the stanzas of "The Star-Spangled Banner," made our National Anthem by Act of Congress in 1931, contains these verses:
>
> > Blest with victory and peace, may the heav'n rescued land
> > Praise the Pow'r that hath made and preserved us a nation!
> > Then conquer we must, when our cause it's just,
> > And this be our motto "In God is our Trust.
>
> In 1954, Congress added a phrase to the Pledge of Allegiance to the Flag so that it now contains the words "one Nation *under God*, indivisible, with liberty and justice for all." In

1952, Congress enacted legislation calling upon the President each year to proclaim a National Day of Prayer. Since 1865, the words "IN GOD WE TRUST" have been impressed on our coins.[11]

Two decades after the initial uproar, the Court strayed even further when it used *Lemon* to invalidate a simple "moment of silence" required by Alabama law. The statute allowed the silent time to be used for voluntary prayer or meditation, and teachers were permitted to lead willing students in prayer to Almighty God. The Supreme Court struck down this law because it had a religious purpose—to return prayer to public schools.[12]

School graduation prayers were banned in 1992, because of psychological coercion—a concern far removed from the persecution in early American colonies that prompted the First Amendment. Middle school principal Lee had invited a rabbi to offer a nonsectarian prayer at the ceremony for 14-year-old Deborah Weisman's graduating class.[13] Under the brand new test for constitutionality created by this decision, a single unbeliever who squirms in the presence of prayer can deprive all of the other students of the comfort and joy of acknowledging God at their graduation.

In 2000, the Court stretched the judicial elastic even further.[14] Mormons and Catholics joined forces to challenge a school district policy allowing a *student*-elected *student* council chaplain to deliver a prayer at high school football games. In striking down the policy, the Supreme Court underscored the school's role. The football games were *school*-sponsored events occurring on *school* property. The invocation was given over the *school's* public address system in an environment supervised by *school* officials where the *school's* name was prominently displayed. The prayer was delivered by a *school* student body representative, but the Court bypassed the role of students, who determined whether an invocation would even be offered, and if so, by whom. The student who was elected—not the school—controlled the content. This unfortunate decision fails to discern the difference between coercion and accommodation.

It's intriguing to compare the school prayer decisions with Pledge of Allegiance cases. In 1940, the Supreme Court ruled against two Jehovah's Witness students who were expelled for their refusal to participate in the mandatory flag-salute and Pledge.[15] The decision was short-lived. Just three years later, the Court reversed itself in another Jehovah's Witness challenge, acknowledging the right to opt out of the compulsory salute and Pledge.[16] Decades later, the Supreme Court sent atheist Michael Newdow packing when he sued over the words "under God," added to the Pledge after the two earlier Pledge rulings. Although Newdow was thrown out on a technicality—he was not his daughter's custodial parent and therefore not the right person to bring the lawsuit—the concurring opinion of Justices Rehnquist, O'Connor, and Thomas provides considerable background about America's religious heritage and affirms the constitutionality of religious expression that is not coerced, like the words "under God" in the Pledge.

The Pledge of Allegiance cases affirm the principle that government may not *coerce* religious expression. Nevertheless, schools *may* include the flag-salute and Pledge in their daily routine so long as there is no improper coercion. Unfortunately, the same principle has not carried over to voluntary student prayer.

## Banning the Bible

In 1642, Massachusetts passed the first compulsory education law, the Old Deluder Satan Law, so that children could learn to read the Bible.[17] Just over three centuries later, American public schools began a dramatic departure from these biblical origins.

Ellery Frank Schempp was a student at Abington Senior High School in Philadelphia in the 1950s. Each school day began with a mandatory reading of ten verses from the King James Bible, followed by recitation of the Lord's Prayer, as required by Pennsylvania law. His family attended a theologically liberal Unitarian denomination and did not accept the teachings of the Bible. Ellery decided to protest. On November 26, 1956, Ellery began silently reading a copy of the Koran while other students listened to the daily Bible verses.[18] Thus began a long legal journey that culminated in the Supreme Court's 1963 decision to ban Bible reading in the public schools.[19] The Court rendered its *Schempp* decision in conjunction with its reversal of a similar case filed in Baltimore, Maryland by atheist activist Madalyn Murray O'Hair—where lower courts had upheld daily Bible reading because students had the option to be excused.[20]

The Ten Commandments have suffered a similar fate. The Commandments undergird much of our judicial system, but *Lemon* has soured courts to allowing them in public school classrooms. Kentucky law once required that the Ten Commandments be posted on the wall of each public school classroom. The Supreme Court invalidated that law in 1980. Although the Commandments can be studied as literature, history, or comparative religion, they are plainly religious, involving not only arguably secular matters but also matters of worship. Even though voluntary contributions were used to buy the posters, and even though no student was forced to read, recite, believe, or follow the Commandments, the Court found that posting them in public school classrooms implied official state support and lacked the secular purpose required by *Lemon*.[21]

## Textbooks, Tests, and Teachers on Trial

An alarming paranoia has swept through American courtrooms. Courts have placed a broad hedge of protection around the Establishment Clause, lest sometime, somewhere, somehow, a nickel of public money might inadvertently slip through the public fingers to advance the cause of religion. To borrow an expression of the apostle Paul: "May it never be!"[22] The Supreme Court has created a confusing hodge-podge of hair-splitting rules about if, when, and how state funds may be used for the benefit of school-age children whose parents choose to enroll them in private religious schools, often (but not always) applying the sour *Lemon* criteria:

- 1930 (pre-*Lemon*): State funds may be used to provide books for private school students because the children benefit rather than the religious schools they attend.[23]
- 1968 (pre-*Lemon*): The state may finance textbooks for children in private schools, because the purpose and primary

effect is to neither advance nor inhibit religion—similar to one prong of the *Lemon* test adopted several years later.[24]

- 1973 (applying *Lemon*): State funds may not be used to maintain or repair nonpublic elementary and secondary schools. The Court also struck down programs for tuition reimbursement and tax deductions.[25]

- 1975 (applying *Lemon*) (partially overruled in 2000): Textbook loans may be made for children in private religious schools, but the state may not finance equipment (projection, recording, laboratory) or instructional materials (periodicals, photographs, maps, charts, sound recordings, films, or any other printed and published materials of a similar nature).[26]

- 1977 (applying *Lemon*) (partially overruled in 2000): State financing for books, standardized testing and scoring, diagnostic services, and therapeutic and remedial services was constitutional *but* provisions for funding of instructional materials, equipment and field trip services were unconstitutional.[27]

- 1980 (applying *Lemon*): The state may reimburse private schools for the costs of a state-prepared testing program.[28]

- 1983 (applying *Lemon*): The Court upheld parental tax deductions for costs associated with private schooling, including tuition, textbooks, and transporation.[29]

- 1985 (applying *Lemon*) (overruled in 1997): The Court struck down a program sending public school teachers into parochial school to provide remedial education, because of excessive entanglement between the state and religion.[30]

- 1985 (applying *Lemon*) (overruled in 1997): A Shared Time program was struck down because it impermissibly endorsed religion.[31]

- 1993 (*Lemon* test *not* applied): A deaf student attending a Catholic school was entitled to a sign-language interpreter under the Individuals with Disabilities Education Act.[32]

- 1997: A federally funded supplemental education program to benefit disadvantaged students, provided on a neutral basis, was constitutional. This case overruled two 1985 cases that invalidated remedial education and Shared Time programs.[33]

- 2000 (applying *Lemon* and partially overruling two earlier cases): The Court upheld provisions in the Education Consolidation and Improvement Act of 1981 that provided equipment and materials to public and private schools. Eligibility was neutrally determined and aid was allocated based on private choices.[34]

- 2002: Tuition aid to private school students and tutorial aid to public school students were based on the choices of private individuals and therefore constitutional.[35]

## *Lemon*-Aid: Government Funding for Construction and Higher Education

The obsession about never funding religion is more relaxed when the financial aid benefits institutions of higher education, where presumably students are not so young and impressionable. Applying the *Lemon* test, the Supreme Court upheld federal construction grants for church-related colleges and universities[36] and a Maryland grant program to church-affiliated colleges using the funds solely for secular educational purposes.[37]

These cases about financial aid may seem academic, but the sheer number of cases and the emphasis on minutia illustrates the Court's ongoing compulsion to maintain the high wall of separation between church and state. This obsession has broad implications for other issues, such as student religious expression and school curriculum.

## Parental Rights and Wrongs

The Supreme Court generally upholds the fundamental right of parents to direct the upbringing of their children, including religious instruction. Many years ago, the Court struck down an Oregon statute compelling children to attend public schools on the grounds that the statute "unreasonably interfere[d] with the liberty of parents and guardians to direct the upbringing of children under their control."[38] Parents are free to send their children to private schools or provide homeschooling. Amish parents achieved a major victory in 1972 when the Court exempted them from otherwise applicable criminal penalties for refusing to send their children to public school beyond the eighth grade. Their religious way of life was severely threatened by the compulsory education law.[39] More recently, the Court overruled the interests of grandparents seeking visitation rights because of its strong interest in protecting parental rights to the control, care, and custody of their children.[40]

But parental rights are not without limitations, even where the *child's* religious faith is implicated and the child is not abused or otherwise at risk. In 1944, the Court upheld the conviction of a Jehovah's Witness for violating child labor laws by taking her nine-year-old niece with her to conduct street evangelism in the evenings. Mrs. Prince and her niece, Betty, believed it was their God-given duty to preach and distribute religious literature in the streets.[41] This ruling might be reasonable if the child were truly in danger, but the Court admitted there were other children in the same area, at the same time, engaged in shopping and other activities.[42]

Although courts acknowledge parental rights in raising their children, grave dangers loom on the horizon as our culture strays further from God's Word. One of the most serious threats is the public school classroom, where children are regularly taught from a corrupted curriculum that omits God and opposes basic biblical truths.

## Curriculum Corrupted

Schools teach *diversity* and *tolerance* but show little *tolerance* for Christian families and their moral values. Similarly, there is *no tolerance* for parents who object to state indoctrination about the origins of man.

David and Tonia Parker were outraged when Jacob, their kindergarten son, brought home a Diversity Book Bag with a picture book, *Who's In A Family?*, showing families with two dads or two moms. There ought to be a law . . . actually there was a state law requiring notice to parents about curriculum concerning human sexuality, but it didn't apply. The Parkers' concerns were dismissed, and when Jacob entered first grade he was exposed to *Molly's Family*, a picture book about a girl with a mommy and a mama.

Young Joey Wirthlin, a second grader at the same school, heard his teacher read *King and King* out loud to his class. The book told the story of a prince who fell in love and married another prince after his mother ordered him to get married, and he rejected several princesses. The last page portrayed the two princes kissing, with a red heart over their mouths. Like the Parkers, Mr. and Mrs. Wirthlin were gravely concerned about what their young son was learning at school.

These distraught parents *lost* in the federal First Circuit Court of Appeals.[43] This outrageous decision found no constitutional burden on these families' rights to religious liberty. Parents have little or nothing to say about the curriculum taught in public schools, even where it's deeply offensive and shoves a radical political agenda down the throats of their unsuspecting little children. Courts zealously guard the *wall* between church and state because young, impressionable children might experience coercion—by reading and obeying, for example, the Ten Commandments. Yet courts reject the argument that parents are entitled to notice when their children are exposed to families with same-sex parents, dismissing the argument that indoctrination is occurring.

The landscape is not improving for our young people. On April 1, 2008, attorneys from Advocates for Faith and Freedom and Alliance Defense Fund filed a state case challenging the constitutionality of a new statute that revised the California Education Code to redefine the term gender for all public schools. [44] *Gender* is now whatever a child thinks he is, regardless of biological make-up.[45] There are potentially disastrous consequences to this law, including the requirement to open the girls' locker room to boys who decide to be girls and the boys' locker room to girls who identify themselves as boys. On the national level, it was alarming to learn that Kevin Jennings, founder of Gay, Lesbian, and Straight Education Network (GLSEN), was appointed Assistant Deputy

Secretary for the Department of Education's Office of Safe & Drug Free Schools.[46] Our schools are anything but safe with the growing influx of pro-homosexual teachings and policies.

Evolution is another hot button topic. America has come a long way since the Scopes' Monkey Trial made headlines.[47] First, the Supreme Court invalidated a law that prohibited the teaching of evolution (1968). Then two decades later, it struck down a law requiring that creation be taught along with evolution to provide balanced teaching.

Arkansas passed a law in 1928 that prohibited teaching evolution in public schools. In 1965, the school administration adopted a biology textbook that taught evolution. Mrs. Epperson, a Little Rock high school biology teacher, found herself in a Catch 22. She could either teach from the text and subject herself to criminal penalties—or refuse to teach from it and risk dismissal. She and several parents initiated litigation. The Supreme Court ultimately struck down the law, ruling that Arkansas could not prohibit the teaching of a particular scientific theory, because of its conflict with the biblical account of creation. The law lacked religious neutrality because it suppressed all teachings about origins that denied God's creation of man. To be constitutional, the curriculum would have had to exclude *all* discussion about the origins of man.[48]

Some years later, after *Lemon* had established criteria to evaluate religious neutrality, the Court would not even uphold a Louisiana law that required the presentation of creation science along with evolutionary theory. No school was required to teach either creation or evolution, but if either one was taught, the other position also had to be presented. The Court rejected arguments about academic freedom—giving students information about both creation and evolution, rather than indoctrinating them to the facts and theory of evolution. The ruling found the law had an impermissible religious purpose—to discredit evolution and promote a particular religious viewpoint.[49] As a result, Christian children attending public schools are now forced to learn a so-called scientific theory diametrically opposed to their faith, while a gag order is imposed on teaching about creation because of its religious nature.

## Things to Think About

As Christians, it's worth asking ourselves some hard questions about these cases. Do we really want our school children to participate in prayer so watered down that it doesn't even address the true God of the Bible? Do we want our children to believe that they can pray with children of other faiths who are actually praying to another god and not the living God of the Bible? Inter-denominational prayers among Christians may be acceptable (Presbyterian, Lutheran, Baptist, etc.) but not inter-*faith* prayers between Christians and Hindus, Buddhists, Muslims. We pray to a different *God*. Do we want to fight to return Bible reading to public schools, if it means exposing our children to the religious texts of other faiths that are likely to flood the classrooms? What if a daily reading from the Koran or the Book of Mormon became mandatory in a particular school district?

At the same time, God is involved in every aspect of life. Religion is not meant to be reserved for one day per week and excised from daily life. God's Word applies to all our thoughts and actions, all week, every day, in every setting. As the Psalmist exclaimed: "O how I love Your law! It is my meditation *all the day*" (Ps. 119:97 ESV, emphasis added). The exclusion of religious expression from public places contributes to a compartmentalization that weakens the witness of God's people in the world. The dangers of idolatry and compromise loom large, but it's also dangerous to relegate religion to a small corner of life. Believers must live *in* the world yet not be *of* the world. God's Word is our constant, faithful guide, whether in prominent visible events or the intimate details of private homes. Scripture exhorts Christians to nurture and instruct their children in biblical truth, and at this time in history that may require a certain degree of withdrawal from public institutions that would draw them away from God's Word. Many believers home school or enroll their young children in private Christian schools. Perhaps this is necessary, but the resulting isolation is sad, because God's people are called to be the "salt and light" of the earth (Matt. 5:13–16) among a "crooked generation" (Phil. 2:15).

In America, we enjoy the freedom *to* worship but we don't live in a theocracy where church and state are inextricably linked. Because of the strong Christian influence in the founding of America, many civil laws are based on biblical principles. The erosion of that foundation is increasingly noticeable in the courts. Murder is still illegal but every woman has the fundamental right to terminate the life of her unborn child. Marriage is still an institution with legal recognition and benefits, but legislatures and courts increasingly acknowledge same-sex unions. The religious landscape of our country has changed dramatically over the past two centuries. Like it or not, we now live in a religiously plural society. The mission field is no longer far across the sea, but right in our own backyards. There are no easy answers as we struggle to maintain a witness and presence in the world yet protect our young people from dangerous, ungodly influences. American may never be the same predominantly Christian nation that it was at its founding, but Jesus Christ is the same yesterday, today, and forever, and He is faithful.

# *Twelve*

# Banishing the Bible in Places of Business

*Indeed, all who desire to live a godly life in Christ Jesus will be persecuted* (2 TIMOTHY 3:12 ESV).

Maureen Loya had been employed for eighteen years as a group counselor at Orangewood Children's Home, a county shelter for abused children in Southern California. One summer day in June 2006, she took four teenage girls on a field trip, first to the Anaheim 5K race featuring a live rock band, then on to the beach, where the Second Annual Surfrider Foundation Celebrity Surf Jam was taking place at the Huntington Beach Pier. While enjoying their pizza at the beach, the girls briefly overheard music from a Christian band. Noise from the ocean and street soon drowned out the music. The group also visited a few arts and crafts booths, some of which had Christian content. No one complained, but Maureen was interrogated a few weeks later and suspended for thirty days for exposing the children to religious content. This was not the first time Maureen was singled out for disciplinary action because of her faith—it was merely the latest incident in a series occurring over several years. In early 2009, Maureen filed suit for unlawful discrimination, and the case is ongoing as this book goes to press.[1]

*C*hristians face many legal hurdles when they express their faith in the workplace. Christian employers may be required to employ persons engaged in sinful lifestyles. Christian employees may face adverse employment decisions for even simple expressions of faith, such as Bible verses displayed in their personal workspace. Both may crash into legal brick walls if they dare to attempt even modest, non-threatening evangelism with fellow workers.

The theological nature of these issues was noted by a perceptive federal judge who dissented from a court ruling against a Christian-owned company:

> The agency and the court appear to assume that there must be a sharp division between secular activity and religious activity. Such a sharp division finds nourishment in one of our cases. *St. Elizabeth Community Hosp. v. NLRB*, 708 F.2d 1436, 1441 (9th Cir. 1983). But of course such a dichotomy is a species of theology. The theological position is that human beings should worship God on Sundays or some other chosen day and go about their business without reference to God the rest of the time. Such a split is attractive to some religious persons. It is repudiated by many, especially those who seek to integrate their lives and to integrate their activities.[2]

The Bible is not silent about the responsibilities of Christian employers and employees. Passages like Eph. 6:5–9, Col. 3:22, 1 Tim. 6:1, and Titus 2:9, while using the words "slave" and "master," establish principles for modern believers who employ or work for others. Biblical standards also apply to the challenges Christians face when confronting sin in the workplace. Particular sins, like homosexuality, are publicly paraded and even legally protected. Believers must be sensitive, gentle, and humble, yet strong in refusing to compromise their faith. Scriptures like Galatians 6:1 provide wise exhortation about humbly restoring those entangled in sin while remembering that we, too, are saved by God's grace and subject to temptation. Christians have legal rights that must sometimes be pursued in order to avoid sin or set precedent for others, but they also have solemn responsibilities before God for their conduct in their workplace.

### *Serving God While Serving Man*—Christian Employees in the Workplace:

> *Slaves [employees], obey your earthly masters [employers] with fear and trembling, with a sincere heart, as you would Christ; not by the way of eyeservice, as people-pleasers, but as servants of Christ, doing the will of God from the heart, rendering service with a good will as to the Lord and not to man, knowing that whatever good anyone does, this he will receive back from the Lord, whether he is a slave or free* (EPHESIANS 6:5–7 ESV).

Employees have significant rights under Title VII of the 1964 Civil Rights Act,[3] including freedom from discrimination, harassment, and hostile working environments, as well as the right to accommodation of their religious beliefs. Some of the earlier religious freedom decisions arose out of employment relationships where job duties conflicted with religious convictions (Chapters 2–3). But with the advent of new legal rights—including abortion and same-sex unions—and the expansion of categories protected from discrimination, the employment context is a fertile breeding ground for litigation. The Christian employee's right to be free of religious discrimination, and to engage in religious expression, easily clashes with newly minted rights such as abortion and freedom from sexual orientation discrimination.

Religious employees seeking accommodation from employers have met with mixed success, either because of substantial hardship to the employer or the growing push to eradicate discrimination against sexually immoral lifestyles. In 1977, the Supreme Court heard a case involving a TWA employee, Hardison, who worked in an airplane maintenance department that operated twemty-four hours a day throughout the year. His religious faith precluded working on Saturdays, but he did not have enough seniority to be able to select satisfactory working hours. He was eventually terminated when an accommodation could not be arranged. The Court upheld the termination, finding it would have been an unreasonable hardship for TWA to accommodate Hardison. TWA would have had to abandon the union's seniority system or pay premium overtime.[4]

The Court affirmed the general principle of accommodation, but it simply did not work in this situation.

A more recent Seventh Circuit case is similar. After Indiana legalized gambling, state police officer Benjamin Endres, a devout Baptist, was assigned to work full-time as a Gaming Commission agent at the Blue Chip Casino. He refused to accept the assignment because of his religious conviction that gambling is sinful and it would be a sin to facilitate it. His employment was terminated. The court rejected his claim that the Indiana State Police had to accommodate his religious objections to the assignment. The job was an unpopular position for which there were not enough officers to volunteer, and the police would have incurred substantial costs to make the requested accommodation.[5]

Other cases are more encouraging. Marita Lotosky, a research nurse in New York, was required to read a consent form to patients explaining the medical need to use birth control while participating in certain drug studies. This created a conflict with her Roman Catholic faith, but the university would not accommodate her and suggested she transfer to another position. She continued reading the forms but was later terminated after she gave a crucifix to a psychotic patient. The court allowed her religious discrimination case to go forward.[6] Similarly, an Orthodox Jew in Florida (Hillel Hellinger) applied for a pharmacist position but was not hired because of his refusal—on religious grounds—to sell condoms. Eckerd learned about Hellinger's religious beliefs from one of his references and decided not to hire him. However, the company could have accommodated his beliefs without undue hardship. It was unlawful for them to decline his application.[7]

There will certainly be heated battle in the courts if same-sex marriage is legalized on a wide scale. Christians employed by government entities and agencies—not to mention those in the private sector—may face grave consequences if they refuse to facilitate the new marriages. Three town clerks unsuccessfully challenged their obligation under Vermont's civil union law to issue a civil union license or appoint an assistant to do so. The Vermont court acknowledged an offense to the clerks' sincerely held religious beliefs but found those beliefs were not substantially burdened by the law because the duty could be referred to an assistant clerk:

> We do not believe, however, that such an indirect and attenuated connection to the subject of the law substantially burdens plaintiffs' rights to freely exercise their religion in any degree approaching constitutional significance. See, e.g., *Curtis v. School Committee of Falmouth*, 420 Mass. 749, 652 N.E.2d 580, 587–89 (Mass. 1995) (availability of, or exposure to, condom distribution program in public schools did not substantially burden objecting parents' or students' free exercise rights "to any degree approaching constitutional dimensions").[8]

Counselors employed by government agencies will also face conflicts of conscience. Sandra Bruff, a graduate of Reformed Theological Seminary with a master's degree in marriage and family counseling, worked for North Mississippi Health Services as one of three employee assistant plan (EAP) counselors. She objected—on religious grounds—to counseling a client about how to improve an extramarital or same-sex relationship. She was willing to counsel the *person*, but not to facilitate the sinful sexual relationship. That would have violated not only her conscience but Mississippi's laws against sodomy. A jury awarded her damages, but the Fifth Circuit Court of Appeals reversed the decision, concluding that her employer could not shift responsibilities without undue hardship.[9]

### *Serving God While Serving Man:* Christian Witness in the Workplace

Believers may also confront obstacles when they express their faith at work. The result may differ depending on whether the employer is a public or private entity.

The Supreme Court considered the free speech rights of public employees in a 2006 case.[10] A public employee wears two hats—one as a private citizen, another as official representative of his government employer. As a citizen, he has First Amendment rights to free speech—including religious speech. But when acting in his official capacity, he is subject to regulations necessary for the public employer's efficient operations. The issue is not necessarily *where* the speech occurs—at work or some other location—but whether the employee is carrying out official duties or speaking as a private person.

Several years ago, the Ninth Circuit considered a lawsuit brought by Monte Tucker, a religious computer analyst who worked for the California Department of Education.[11] In his zeal to give glory to God, Tucker began placing the acronym SOTLJC after his name on the label of a software program he was working on. SOTLJC stood for Servant of the Lord Jesus Christ. His supervisors objected and gave him several instructions. First, he was to cease placing religious acronyms or symbols on company documents. Tucker accepted this ban. But second, he was ordered not to engage in *any* written or oral religious advocacy at the workplace or during work hours, and third, he was told not to display or store *any* religious literature beyond the small sphere of his work cubicle. The court found the last two restrictions far too broad, impermissibly infringing Tucker's First Amendment rights as a private citizen.

Expressions about homosexuality have met with mixed results in both the public and private employment spheres. Sexual orientation has become a legally protected classification, and that protection collides with biblical expression.

One important principle emerged in an Eighth Circuit case involving the Minnesota Department of Corrections:[12] If employees don't take required diversity training seriously, the employer cannot single out religious objectors for punishment and ignore other inattentive employees. Three Christian employees (Thomas Altman, Kristen Larson, and Kenneth Yackly) silently read their Bibles and copied Scripture during a mandatory seventy-five-minute presentation about "Gays and Lesbians in the Workplace." They all received written reprimands rendering them ineligible for promotion. The federal court of appeals did not find the mandatory training program to be a substantial burden on the employees' religion, even though these three Christians had read the materials in advance and concluded the training session would be state-sponsored indoctrination designed to sanction an immoral lifestyle contrary to the Bible. But they were treated unequally, and that is what the court highlighted in its favorable decision. Other employees had slept or read magazines but were not disciplined.

Christian employees in the Ninth Circuit lost when their public employer removed their pro-family flyer.[13] Judith Jennings, a lesbian employed by the Oakland Community and Economic Development Agency, complained when she saw a flyer posted on the office bulletin board by two employees belonging to the Good News Employee Association, a forum for people of faith to express themselves on contemporary marriage and family issues. The flyer, calling on workers to Preserve Our Workplace with Integrity, promoted the association and its views about marriage, family values, and the natural family. Jennings said she was very uncomfortable and anxious working with people who held such views. The flyer was taken down. The Court upheld the employer's action in removing the flyer, finding it had an interest in preventing workplace disruption and observing that the Good News employees were free to share their views during break periods or outside the workplace. Unlike the Eighth Circuit *Altman* case, this case involved a homosexual employee voicing objections to Christian expression. She might have sued the employer for creating a hostile working environment if the flyer had not been removed.

In the private sphere, victories are rare when believers voice their views about homosexuality in a company that promotes diversity. Richard Peterson, a Hewlett Packard employee whose job performance had been satisfactory for twenty-one years, was fired for insubordination when he refused to remove Scriptures he had posted in his work cubicle. Hewlett Packard held a three-day diversity conference in Boise, Idaho in 1997, and then developed a diversity campaign. The company began to display diversity posters, including the picture of a gay employee. In protest, Peterson posted two Bible verses (Isa. 3:9, 1 Cor. 10:12) in his work cubicle that were visible to those passing through an adjacent corridor. His purpose was to witness to homosexual co-workers. But when he posted Lev. 20:13 (a verse condemning homosexuality), his supervisors demanded he remove it because it might offend certain employees and violated the company's anti-harassment policy: "Any comments or conduct relating to a person's race, gender, religion, disability, age, sexual orientation, or ethnic background that fail to respect the dignity and feeling [sic] of the individual are unacceptable."[14] The Court upheld the discharge, reasoning that Peterson was terminated for insubordination and not because of his religious beliefs. The court also held that it would create undue hardship for Hewlett Packard to accommodate Peterson by allowing him to post messages intended to demean and harass his co-workers or to exclude homosexuals from its voluntarily-adopted diversity program. The court also affirmed Hewlett Packard's goal of eradicating discrimination against homosexuals as being consistent with civil rights statutes generally.

Christians employed by General Motors protested the company policy of recognizing affinity groups for gay employees but not religious employees. GM had adopted an affinity recognition program to support employees from diverse groups and increase productivity, but religious groups were not included. John Moranski, a desktop computer architect, submitted an application for the Christian Employee Network to join the program, but it was denied. He lost his claim to religious discrimination, because *all* religious groups were excluded and GM is a private entity not subject to the First Amendment.[15] Although the result and the Court's pro-homosexual attitude are disappointing, the legal principle cuts both ways. If the Court had reached the opposition conclusion, a private company owned by Christians might be required to recognize gay groups if it adopted an affinity program. Moreover, mandating recognition of the Christian group would undoubtedly necessitate allowing non-Christian religious groups.

There is a glimmer of light at the end of this tunnel. As one court ruling illustrates, an employer cannot coerce an employee to affirm or value another person's sexual expression. AT&T employee, Buonanno, refused to sign an antidiscrimination policy that required him to value the beliefs of his employer and co-workers: "Each person at AT&T Broadband is charged with the responsibility to fully recognize, respect and value the differences among all of us."[16] Buonanno was a Christian willing to value and respect all other AT&T employees as persons, but he could not endorse or approve behaviors or values condemned by Scripture. After consultation with his pastor and one Christian supervisor, he attempted to resolve the conflict through a letter and meeting with supervisors, but instead was terminated. AT&T failed to offer a reasonable accommodation, clarify the ambiguous language, or resolve the conflict which was not the policy itself, but rather the requirement that Buonanno value the beliefs of others, even if those beliefs conflicted with his own religious convictions. Buonanno's respectful but uncompromising letter to AT&T is a wonderful model for believers to emulate as they courageously respond to similar challenges in the workplace:

> I can't comply with the ambiguous statement under 'Diversity' on pages six and seven [of the Handbook]. . . As an AT&T employee I am fully cognizant of the fact that there is diversity among its members. Since being hired on January 10, 1999, I have indiscriminately conducted myself in a professional manner with all people. . . . However, . . . *I believe it's wrong for any individual or organization to attempt to persuade me to fully respect and fully value any differences which are contrary to God's word. In order for me to comply with this diversity statement in the company handbook, I would have to deny my faith; this I will not do.* It is this reason that prohibits me from signing the certificate of acknowledgment. . . .As an AT&T employee I give you my word that I will continue to conduct myself in the same professional manner. But I can't allow any group or individual to choose for me what I must respect or place value on.[17]

## *Hiring and Holiness:* Christian Employers in the Workplace

> *Masters [employers], do the same to them [your employees], and stop your threatening, knowing that He who is both their Master and yours is in heaven, and that there is no partiality with Him* (EPHESIANS 6:9 ESV).

Well-intentioned Christian entrepreneurs sometimes want to saturate their business atmospheres with expressions of faith. There are limits to what they can do without trampling the legal rights of customers and employees. Jake and Helen Townley, owners of an engineering company based in Florida, made a covenant with God to maintain a Christian, faith-operated business, based on their conviction that God could not be separated from any portion of their lives. They enclosed gospel tracts with every piece of outgoing company mail, printed Bible verses on company documents (letterhead, invoices, purchase orders), gave financial support to churches and missionaries, and held weekly devotional services during business hours. All employees were required to attend. Louis Pelvas, an atheist, came to work for the company as a machinist. He objected to the required devotionals and sued. The court held that the Townleys were free to hold company-sponsored prayer meetings but could not mandate attendance.[18]

Christian business owners in Minnesota held similar convictions about integrating faith and business. Marc Crevier and Forest Larson owned and operated seven sports and health clubs. These two Christians believed they should operate their business in accordance with the will of God and teachings of Jesus Christ. When interviewing prospective employees, they asked questions about religious beliefs, church attendance, and sexual conduct. They would only hire Christians as managers or assistant managers, based on their understanding of 2 Cor. 6:14–18. Weekly Bible studies comprised part of the weekly managers' meetings, and voluntary Bible studies were offered for sales people. The owners refused to hire or continue the employment of persons who engaged in sexual sin—including homosexuality. In a lawsuit involving multiple plaintiffs, the court found their practices to be unlawful discrimination.[19]

Homosexual employees terminated by individual religious supervisors have successfully initiated lawsuits for discrimination, harassment, and/or hostile working environment. Plaintiff Del Erdmann, a homosexual, was employed by San Miguel Villa, a California nursing home. He alleged that supervisor Velda Pierce, a Mormon, discriminated against him and created a hostile, abusive work environment because of her religious belief that homosexuality is immoral. There were prayer meetings conducted at the job site. Pierce told Erdmann that his homosexual life style was immoral and that he would go to hell. She also told him that other employees were uncomfortable with his homosexuality because homosexuals are promiscuous—and therefore, she instructed him to tell the other employees that he was currently engaged in a monogamous relationship and did not want to become involved with any of his co-workers. The court allowed this case to go forward, denying the employer's request to kick the case.[20]

A lawsuit in New York not only went forward—but the supervisor was ordered to answer questions about his religious faith. John Fairchild, a homosexual, alleged that Ted Doudak, his supervisor at Riva Jewelry Manufacturing, fired him because of his sexual orientation in violation of New York state and local antidiscrimination laws. Doudak quoted Scripture often and expressed his disgust with homosexuality. One day, Doudak noticed a lesbian magazine on Fairchild's desk and asked him about it. Fairchild had purchased it for his lesbian daughter, and he revealed to Doudak that he and his daughter were both homosexuals. Doudak quoted Scripture and told Fairchild that homosexuals were doomed to eternal damnation, then terminated Fairchild the next day without a legitimate business reason. As the lawsuit progressed, Fairchild asked questions about Doudak's religious *beliefs—going beyond his actual statements*—to support his claim that allegations of poor work performance were merely a pretext for the real motivation behind his discharge—his sexual orientation. The court required the employer to answer the questions, which included:

- State whether defendant Doudak believes that "homosexuality is a sin against God."
- State whether defendant Doudak believes that "gays and lesbians are doomed to eternal damnation."
- State whether defendant Doudak regards homosexuals as "repulsive."[21]

We might well disagree with this supervisor's attitude and manner of presenting biblical truth. But it's frightening to see how religious beliefs can be used in a court of law to establish legal liability to a person whose sexual perversion is the basis for his protected legal status. Moreover, there is an ominous statement near the end of the decision that reflects the increasingly popular belief that sexual orientation trumps religious liberty:

It is the duty of every Court to guard jealously the great right and privilege of free exercise and enjoyment of religious profession and worship without discrimination or preference, with all the power that the Court possesses but *no person should be permitted to use that right as a cloak for acts of discrimination* or as a justification of practices inconsistent with the protections against, invidious discrimination proscribed in New York State law.[22]

On a more positive note, there are some outside limits to the ability of homosexuals to strong-arm employers. The right to employment does not include the right to erect a political platform at the employer's expense. A university library failed to hire a gay librarian after media coverage of his attempt to marry another man. The applicant sought more than employment. His complaint unveiled his plan to seek "the right to pursue an activist role in implementing his unconventional ideas concerning the societal status to be accorded homosexuals and, thereby, to foist tacit approval of this socially repugnant concept upon his employer . . ."[23] An individual in a protected category seeking employment only has the right to be employed for pay, not the right to convert the position into a platform to promote an agenda.

Restrictions on employee conduct are permissible if they are related to qualifications for the job or necessary for the employer's business. For example, the Omaha Girls Club was justified in terminating a black female employee who became pregnant out of wedlock—even though this had a disparate impact on black employees and would normally be considered discriminatory— because the whole purpose of the employer's program was to discourage unmarried black girls from becoming pregnant out of wedlock, and employees needed to be appropriate role models.[24]

The greatest legal protection is granted to churches, church affiliates (such as schools), and sometimes other religious organizations— behind church doors. That is the subject of our next chapter.

# *Thirteen*

# Behind
# Church Doors

*A prudent man sees danger and takes refuge, but the simple keep
going and suffer for it* (PROVERBS 22:3 NIV).

> In 1980, years before the homosexual agenda made national headlines,
> a small Orthodox Presbyterian Church in San Francisco terminated a gay
> church organist for failure to repent and comply with the church's moral
> standards. The organist sued the church under a city ordinance forbidding
> sexual orientation discrimination in employment. The church ultimately
> prevailed, but only after protracted litigation.[1]

*R*eligious expression should be safe in the sanctuary, but it's
not necessarily so. Houses of worship must have their legal
houses in order to reasonably minimize risks and respond to any
legal challenges that do occur. Governing documents should be
well drafted with careful attention to religious doctrine. Employment policies should be consistent with church teachings and
uniformly applied. Shepherding God's flock, through pastoral
counseling and church discipline, must never compromise God's

Word—nevertheless, pastors need to keep one eye on the courts in this age of litigation, because "sheep" can sue.

## Hands Off!

Courts are generally reluctant to become embroiled in theological controversies. That hesitation—grounded in the First Amendment—is an important protection for churches. Churches are not immune from all liability, but courts are rightly cautious about opening church doors.

Case law reflects respect for voluntary religious associations. This is apparent in a couple of cases in the 1880s about the not-so-harmonious Harmony Society, an association established in 1805 by George Rapp and other German immigrants. Members pooled their financial resources, but the association's articles provided that a member could withdraw and claim his share of the community property. One member left the group with his two-hundred-dollar share and then sued, claiming he was harshly treated and unjustly excluded from the society. The court threw his case out.[2] About thirty years later, another disgruntled member of the Harmony Society sued, some *fifty years after* his withdrawal, wanting a share of the millions of dollars the association had accumulated. There were allegations that the founder, George Rapp, had falsely and fraudulently induced people into the association by threatening eternal damnation if they failed to join. Courts are loathe to become involved in disputes about religious doctrine. Moreover, this ex-member had slept on his legal rights—whatever they might be—for too many years. The Court refused to grant him any relief.

Courts sometimes apply general contract law in cases involving religious associations. In the early 1900s, a deceased priest's administrator asserted estate ownership of the copyrights for his published works—but lost. The priest had belonged to the Order of St. Benedict. According to the Order's constitution, he renounced all personal property rights and conveyed everything he owned to the Order. He could withdraw his membership any time and enjoyed some rights to collect income while he was alive. The Supreme

Court upheld the priest's voluntary agreement to transfer his personal property, including copyrights, to the Order.[3]

Several cases illustrate another important principle. On matters of religious doctrine, courts defer to the highest authority in a particular denomination. Often that internal church decision will determine the outcome of disputes over property or personnel.

After the Civil War, the General Assembly of the Presbyterian Church condemned slavery and declared that anyone who aided that war of rebellion would be ineligible for membership, ministry, or missionary work. A new General Assembly was organized in the South to preserve slavery. The Walnut Street Presbyterian Church split and so did the Louisville Presbytery. The Supreme Court concluded it was bound by the General Assembly's decision as to which faction constituted the "true" church.[4]

Presbyterian property rights emerged in the Court again a century later. Two Georgia congregations withdrew from the PCUSA denomination because of internal disagreement over the ordination of women and neo-orthodox teachings. One group contended it could withdraw from the denomination and was entitled to retain church property after the break. This conclusion was based on the departure by the denomination from the doctrinal standard that provided the policy whereby the general church abandoned the fundamental tenets of faith and practice,. The two Georgia congregations voted to withdraw from the PCUSA and form their own autonomous Presbyterian organization. State courts ruled in their favor but the Supreme Court reversed. There was no general church decision that the denomination had departed from the faith. Moreover, the departure from doctrine standard was found unconstitutional in the civil court context because it improperly requires the court to decide issues of religious doctrine.[5]

Judicial deference to the church extends beyond American borders. A New York statute attempted to free the Russian Orthodox Church in America from ecclesiastical control in Moscow, granting it title to St. Nicholas Cathedral in the United States. American-born members of the church were increasingly distant from the religious hierarchy in Russia and wanted to separate, particularly in view of the atheist political climate in Russia. But the statute was contrary to the Supreme Church Authority of the Patriarch of Moscow. The Supreme Court found the state statute unconstitutional because it interfered with church authority.[6] Courts may determine the property rights of religious organizations according to neutral principles of law, but neither the legislature nor a civil court may adjudicate such rights by overruling an internal church decision.

## Hands Off Our Hiring

Courts virtually *never* become involved in church decisions about hiring and firing ministers—who should be ordained, who may preach from the pulpit, or who may participate in worship. Deference to church decisions reaches its apex here. Courts call this the ministerial exception to the general rules about wrongful termination. If a minister is unhappy about losing his position, he will find no recourse in the civil courts—no matter how egregious or unfair the termination may have been.

The Supreme Court considered this issue in 1976. The Eastern Orthodox "mother church" in Yugoslavia suspended and later defrocked Bishop Milivojevich—a controversial figure—after he refused to recognize the suspension. The defrocked bishop believed the Holy Assembly and Holy Synod to be pro-communist. The Illinois Supreme Court ordered his reinstatement, claiming that prescribed church procedure was not followed. The Supreme Court reversed, finding this was improper judicial interference with decisions of the highest authority of a hierarchical church.[7]

The "hands off" policy applies even where the minister is employed by a church affiliate, such as a school. A male homosexual ("Doe") employed by Lutheran High School sued the school and the Lutheran Church-Missouri Synod when his employment was terminated because of his sexual orientation. The high school's faculty handbook and bylaws reflected the religious nature of the school, and the synod had formally recognized that homosexual behavior is sinful. Doe was ordained by the synod in 1976 and worked at the school as a campus pastor. He was also a teacher and chairman of the theology department. He was married with two daughters, but in 1998 he came out and identified himself to his family as a homosexual. His employment termination followed. The court upheld his discharge because it would violate the First Amendment to interfere with the internal governance of a religious organization.[8]

The ministerial exception stretches a little further than the pulpit to cover others involved in religious worship. The gay organist case (*Walker*) at the beginning of this chapter is an example. The Orthodox Presbyterian Church considers its organist an integral part of the *worship* team, based on Scriptures such as Ps. 92, Ps. 81, Col. 3:16, and Eph. 5:19–20. Its doctrine does not permit unrepentant sinners to participate in the worship service. It would have infringed the church's First Amendment rights to allow the organist's suit to proceed on the basis of San Francisco's city ordinance prohibiting discrimination against homosexuals.[9]

A more recent case demonstrates the same principle all over again with a homosexual music minister employed by Mariners Church in Southern California. Robert Gunn was terminated from his position as worship director after church leaders learned of his homosexuality. The senior pastor made an announcement to the congregation—normal church procedure under these circumstances. Most of the statements involved religious doctrine, but the pastor made one factual statement that Gunn disputed—that the leadership had asked him forty or fifty times whether he was homosexual, and he lied in response. Without the ministerial exception, Gunn's case could have gone forward on charges of defamation. But the California appellate court held that Gunn—like the organist in *Walker*—was part of the worship team and thus subject to the ministerial hands off policy.[10]

Even beyond hiring for the worship team, church employers may engage in *religious* discrimination—unlike their secular counterparts—and may require employees to comply with standards of conduct consistent with religious doctrine.

Adrea Boyd was employed as a preschool teacher by Harding Academy, a religious school affiliated with the Church of Christ. All faculty members were required to be Christians. Boyd was terminated when she became pregnant out of wedlock, and the school prevailed when she sued them.[11]

However, beware: If a female employee is discharged for extra-marital sex, it must not be a pretext for *pregnancy*. Leigh Cline was an eighth grade teacher at St. Paul Elementary and High School, a Roman Catholic school. Her employment contract was not renewed because the school learned she was pregnant and had engaged in premarital sex. She sued for sex discrimination, which includes pregnancy. The court framed the relevant issue:

> The central question in this case . . . is whether St. Paul's non-renewal of Cline's contract constituted discrimination based on her pregnancy as opposed to a gender-neutral enforcement of the school's premarital sex policy.[12]

Moreover, churches that terminate unmarried pregnant women must apply comparable standards to men in order to avoid charges of gender discrimination, and the difficulties in proof are obvious. An unmarried elementary school math teacher in New York was terminated because she engaged in sexual intercourse outside of marriage, contrary to the church-affiliated school's religious doctrine. The First Amendment allows religious schools to restrict hiring to those who hold beliefs conforming to the school's doctrine and to fire those who don't act in compliance with it. But limits on sexual conduct cannot be enforced unequally on male and female employees.[13]

Churches and their affiliates also enjoy substantial protection from antidiscrimination laws protecting homosexuals. This is particularly true where ministerial employees are involved, as in the *Walker* and *Gunn* cases, but protection extends to other church employees.

Glynda Hall, a lesbian, was employed as a Student Services Specialist by Baptist Memorial College of Health Sciences. The college is affiliated with the Southern Baptist Convention, which teaches that homosexuality is sin. She belonged to Holy Trinity Community Church, which actively solicits homosexual members and teaches that the homosexual lifestyle is compatible with Christianity. The President of the college asked Hall to resign when her homosexuality was discovered. She sued—but lost—because this religious educational institution was exempt from the prohibition against religious discrimination.[14]

Christine Madsen, a lesbian, was employed by the Christian Science Monitor as a journalist. After several years of employment, she learned that rumors were circulating that she lived with a homosexual, had entered into a homosexual marriage, attended meetings with homosexuals, and had attempted to entice the manager's wife into a homosexual relationship. She denied these allegations except to admit she was gay. Her employment was terminated. She sued the Monitor but lost because the newspaper was a religious activity of the Christian Science Church and she was a church employee. The court had to defer to the church's decision to fire her because it was based on religious doctrine, protected by the First Amendment.[15]

## *Hands Off Our Land:* Federal Protections for Religious Land Use

Faith Fellowship Foursquare Church is bursting at the seams. Neighbors and even church attendees complain about crowded conditions in the residential area where the church meets. Church leaders thought they had solved the problem when they located a large vacant office building in an industrial area. It was big enough for the growing congregation and rarely used on weekends. But the City of San Leandro denied the church's rezoning request because the property could be used to generate jobs and tax revenue. The site allows all sorts of other activities—concerts and even adult entertainment—but bans worship. The church is now represented by the Pacific Justice Institute and headed for the Ninth Circuit Court of Appeals, after U.S. District Judge Phyllis Hamilton suggested that the church split its congregation and conduct activities at multiple locations.[16] The church's appeal is based on protections granted by RLUIPA: *Religious Land Use and Institutionalized Persons Act*, passed by a unanimous Congress in 2000.[17] The first small section of the law is worth reading and remembering, in case your church is ever faced with a negative government decision about the use of church land:

(1) General rule. No government shall impose or implement a land use regulation in a manner that imposes a substantial burden on the religious exercise of a person, including a religious assembly or institution, unless the government demonstrates that imposition of the burden on that person, assembly, or institution—

(A) is in furtherance of a compelling governmental interest; and

(B) is the least restrictive means of furthering that compelling governmental interest.[18]

The government needs a *very* good reason to deny your church's zoning request or otherwise restrict your church's use of its own land, and generating tax revenue from for-profit businesses is not likely to pass muster.

## Shepherding God's Flock: *Sheep v. Shepherd* in the Courts

Jesus told Peter—*three times*—to feed His sheep (John 21:15–17). Both the Old and New Testaments direct pastors to shepherd God's flock, even when it's inconvenient, costly, or threatening (e.g., Jer. 3:15; Ezek. 34:1–10; Acts 20:17–38; 1 Pet. 5:1–4). Sheep are not always grateful for the care they receive, and in today's litigious society sometimes they sue. Human shepherds are also sinners, so at times their shepherding is tainted with sin.

There is potential for litigation in the ministries of pastoral counseling and church discipline (Matt. 18:15–20). We can only hit the highlights, as this huge subject could fill another volume. Pastors and elders need not—indeed should not—shirk biblical responsibilities for fear of lawsuits. But church leaders can be prudent and take preventive steps to resolve conflicts before they explode. Communication, consent, and accountability are important keys in this process, as some court cases illustrate.

Communication is critical to avoiding confusion and conflicts in counseling situations. A written consent form and statement of policies can provide needed clarification. People need to know what you *are* doing and what you *are not* doing.

The First Amendment can provide protection for your *religious* counseling based on Scripture, but it can be lost if a pastor holds himself out to a congregant as a psychotherapist or secular counselor.[19] Penny Penley was having marital troubles and consulted C. L. Westbrook, Jr., a licensed professional marriage counselor who attended her church, McKinney Memorial Bible Church. About a year after their initial counseling sessions, Westbrook, Penley, Penley's husband, and others broke off from McKinney Church and formed CrossLand Community Bible Church, where Westbrook served as its first pastor and elder. All church members were required to sign an affirmation of their willingness to abide by the church's constitution, which included a disciplinary policy. The policy provided for membership to be revoked, with an appropriate announcement to the congregation, in cases of unrepentant sin. Penley and her husband began counseling sessions with Westbrook as their pastor, but ultimately divorced. Penley admitted to adultery. Church discipline followed, including notice to the congregation. She sued the church, its elders, and Westbrook—based on his former role as her professional secular counselor. A Texas appellate court allowed her malpractice case to go forward, but the Texas Supreme Court reversed, explaining that:

> In his dual capacity, Westbrook owed Penley conflicting duties; as Penley's counselor he owed her a duty of confidentiality, and as her pastor he owed Penley and the church an obligation to disclose her conduct. We conclude that parsing those roles for purposes of determining civil liability in this case, where health or safety are not at issue, would unconstitutionally entangle the court in matters of church governance and impinge on the core religious function of church discipline.[20]

The First Amendment protected this pastor and church, but only after an extended journey through the state courts.

Reporting duties under state law are yet another trap for the unwary. Every state law has child abuse reporting requirements, and pastors may learn about such abuse during counseling. Some states provide an exemption for clergy, but if not, the First Amendment will not spare you. Two California pastors learned this lesson the hard way when their *criminal* convictions were affirmed.[21] A teenage girl's stepfather, a minister in the church, was molesting one of the teenage girls attending their church school. These two pastors believed they had to follow scriptural principles and handle the situation within the church. They considered the molestation to be sin rather than sexual abuse. The stepfather had to confess in front of the entire congregation, and he lost his ministerial license. However, the pastors were convicted for failing to report the abuse, and the child abuse reporting statute was found constitutional over their religious objections.

There might also be a duty to warn third parties about plausible threats from a counselee. Some years ago, the California Supreme Court held a licensed psychologist liable when his patient, Prosenjit Poddar, threatened to murder his ex-girlfriend, Tatian Tarasoff—and carried out that threat two months later.[22] The court held that the counselor should have warned Ms. Tarasoff of the specific threat against her life. It's uncertain whether a pastor would be held to the same standard, and state laws can vary widely. Nevertheless, it's something to consider including in your counseling policy.

Most courts have rejected suits for clergy malpractice because it would require them to establish a consistent standard applicable to every religious order. This would improperly entangle the state in religious doctrine. A widely publicized case in California in the late 1980s (*Nally v. Grace Community Church*) is often cited for this principle. Kenneth Nally was active at Grace Community Church for several years. The church had no formal counseling center, but Nally received informal pastoral counseling from Pastor John MacArthur and others. Sadly, he became increasingly despondent and eventually shot himself in the head. After his suicide, his family sued the church. The church was ultimately absolved of legal liability. The California Supreme Court kicked out the malpractice claim and held that the church had no legal duty to refer Nally to a mental health professional. Imposing such a duty would be unconstitutional because it would require secular courts to become embroiled in religious doctrine. Moreover, it would stifle gratuitous and/or religious counseling, discouraging people from seeking spiritual counsel. But nine years elapsed between Nally's

1979 death and the 1988 court ruling.[23] Clear communication with people about the nature of pastoral counseling, and evidence of voluntary consent, can help avoid litigation.

There are limits to First Amendment protection. Many sad cases attest to the tragic results of sexual involvement between a pastor/counselor and counselee. Since religious doctrine does not require such conduct—on the contrary, it is sin—the First Amendment offers no shield to legal liability. Some courts reason that there is no legal case where consenting adults become involved,[24] but others allow suits to go forward.

Steven and Diane Odenthal consulted their Minnesota pastor, Lowell Rideout, for marital counseling. About a year later, Diane and Pastor Rideout—but not Steven—attended an out-of-town church seminar where others observed them acting inappropriately in a motel room. Eventually, Steven and Diane divorced. Pastor Rideout resigned, divorced his wife, and married Diane. Steven, the rejected husband, sued the church and pastor. His suit was allowed to proceed, based on Minnesota's convoluted statutory scheme governing "unlicensed mental health practitioners," as well as the pastor's representation that he could provide marital therapy.[25]

There are many variations on this theme—sometimes an injured husband sues a pastor and church over a wife's infidelity (as in *Odenthal* above), sometimes the couple reconciles and sues,[26] and other times a sexually unfaithful counselee goes to court alleging a pastor's breach of trust for becoming involved with her.[27] Such cases erode the church's testimony when they hit secular courtrooms (see 1 Cor. 6:1–8). The potential for these disastrous situations can be minimized using strong accountability policies and written agreements to resolve disputes through mediation inside the church.

Sexual immorality is not the only limitation to First Amendment protection. The pulpit cannot be used as a pretext for defamation or other wrongful—*sinful*—conduct such as intentional infliction of emotional distress. Harold and Hazel Hester were not church members, but they invited Baptist Pastor Donald Barnett into their home to assist them with the discipline of their children.

He promised confidentiality. Later, he not only betrayed their confidence—he also lied to neighbors and business associates about their conduct. He publicly apologized for these lies but continued to spread them and refused to retract the false statements he had made to the public. If the Hesters had been church members who voluntarily submitted to the church's disciplinary system, some of the pastor's statements might have been protected—but probably not his deliberate lies, which injured their reputations.[28]

Church discipline is integrally related to pastoral counseling and the issues often overlap. As court cases illustrate, it's vitally important that church members understand their church's discipline policy and voluntarily consent to it when they join.

When Marian Guinn and her children moved to the small town of Collinsville, Oklahoma in 1974, they began attending and soon joined the local Church of Christ. Other members reached out and supported her emotionally and financially. But a few years later, church elders learned of her ongoing affair with a man in Collinsville who did not belong to the church—and who was not her husband. They confronted her several times about her sin over many months (Matt. 18:15–17), but the relationship continued. Eventually an announcement was made to the church—*after* she had voluntarily resigned her membership and *after* her attorney had written to the church demanding that they not publicly disclose details of her private life. Guinn sued, went to trial, and a jury awarded damages. On appeal, the court held that the actions of the elders *prior to Guinn's voluntary withdrawal* were protected under the First Amendment, but they were liable for continuing the disciplinary process after she withdrew.[29] Courts generally respect the rights of religious associations. People who join a church consent to its policies and procedures, such as church discipline. Consent may even be implied when a person regularly attends and participates in church functions.[30] But church members have a legal right to withdraw unless there has been a voluntary waiver of that right. If your church believes that discipline must be continued even after a person renounces membership, it's vital that all church members understand and consent to that policy.

## Putting God's House in Order: Articles, Bylaws, and Other Governing Documents

Don't ever be deceived into thinking that "no one would sue a church." People sue churches all the time, tarnishing our witness and draining resources that should be poured into ministry. The Bible provides the wisdom we need to resolve conflicts peacefully, but sometimes people resort to civil courts instead. Occasionally the judicial system must be used where there is no other way, but this should be rare. Meanwhile, church leaders can take action to prevent litigation before it ever happens.

Carefully drafted governing documents (Articles of Incorporation, Bylaws, Constitutions, Books of Church Order) and written policies for discipline, counseling, employment, child care, and other ministries, will help put a hedge of protection around your sanctuary. Contracts for employment, counseling, and other matters can include provisions to mediate disputes within the church and avoid going before secular courts.[31] Most importantly, your church doctrine should be set forth clearly, with references to Scripture.

It is wise, and well worth the financial investment, to retain a local attorney who can guide your church in drafting documents, helping you comply with local law, and handling any legal problems that do arise. Prevention is far less expensive than litigation. If you don't have a qualified attorney in your congregation and funds are tight, you might consider contacting an organization like the Alliance Defense Fund. ADF allies are attorneys who have attended a Christian Litigation Academy through the generosity of donors. These Christian lawyers have made pro bono commitments that could be fulfilled by helping your church.

# Fourteen

# The High Cost of
# Free Speech

*And now, Lord, consider their threats and enable Your servants
to speak Your word with great boldness* (ACTS 4:29 NIV).

*Let your speech always be gracious, seasoned with salt, so that
you may know how you ought to answer each person* (COLOSSIANS
4:6 ESV).

Every spring, the Gay, Lesbian, and Straight Education Network (GLSEN)
sponsors a Day of Silence"in public schools to endorse and promote
homosexual conduct. In response, Christian students have organized a
Day of Truth for the following school day. In April 2004, sixteen-year-
old Chase Harper, a Poway High School sophomore in California, was
suspended and told to "leave his faith in the car"—merely for wearing a
t-shirt expressing the biblical view of homosexuality.[1] It required action
by the U.S. Supreme Court to affirm this courageous young man's freedom to speak biblical truth peacefully.[2] Similar censorship awaits those
who dare to speak about other hot button issues.

*a*mericans have always had the right to free speech. Now it's risky to speak out against legally protected sins or to verbalize the Christian faith in public. Attacks on free speech are legion. Sometimes they're based on the controversial nature of the topic. Other times, the speech occurs at a school or other place where some restrictions are constitutional. Even the identity of the speaker can be a factor—a confusing maze of IRS regulations leaves churches and charities in a fog about what they can say without jeopardizing their tax-exempt status. Threats to free speech lurk behind deceptively worded regulations like the fairness doctrine that is anything but *fair*. Elaborate campaign finance laws stifle speech about political candidates and pending laws right when people most need information.

## Pro-Life Protests, Pickets, Papers, and Parades

In May 2009, Dr. George Tiller, provider of late-term abortions, was shot to death while attending services at Reformation Lutheran Church in Wichita, Kansas. Operation Rescue issued a statement condemning the shooting:

> We are shocked at this morning's disturbing news that Mr. Tiller was gunned down. Operation Rescue has worked for years through peaceful, legal means, and through the proper channels to see him brought to justice. We denounce vigilantism and the cowardly act that took place this morning. We pray for Mr. Tiller's family that they will find comfort and healing that can only be found in Jesus Christ.[3]

When the Supreme Court decided *Casey* in 1992, it made the amazing claim that it could not overrule *Roe* because that case involved an "intensely divisive controversy" requiring the Court to call on the contending sides "to end their national division by accepting a common mandate rooted in the Constitution."[4] There could hardly be a more inaccurate description of the American public's reaction to *Roe*. National controversy has escalated and passions are inflamed on both sides.

The pro-life movement responded to *Roe* in spades. Protesters surround abortion clinics to protest and persuade. Crisis pregnancy centers have sprung up around the country to assist young women with alternatives to abortion. But the issue is explosive and there are also efforts to restrain pro-life enthusiasm. A series of Supreme Court decisions have clarified—and sometimes confused—the legal standards. A multitude of lower court decisions add to this cacophony.

Massachusetts Citizens for Life, a pro-life nonprofit corporation, distributed a special election newsletter to urge pro-life votes and provide information about the positions of candidates without expressly endorsing any of them. This group had to engage in battle over the application of complicated federal campaign finance laws prohibiting corporate expenditures in connection with a federal election. In 1986, the Supreme Court examined the application of the election laws and held that they violated MCFL's free speech rights.[5] This was a pro-life victory, but, as we will see later in the chapter, nonprofit organizations face a confusing maze of restrictions on their right to free speech in the political realm.

The town of Brookfield, Wisconsin enacted an ordinance that prohibited picketing in residential areas. Several individuals opposed to abortion violated this local law when they picketed on a public street outside the home of an abortion doctor. Even though public streets have historically been open to free speech, the Supreme Court upheld this restriction on residential privacy. The picketing targeted a single home, where people inside were essentially a captive audience"[6] This case illustrates the principle that government can place reasonable restrictions on the time, place, and manner of speech, so long as the law does not target a particular viewpoint and alternate channels of communication remain open.

Operation Rescue and other pro-life advocates organized demonstrations around abortion clinics in the Washington, D.C. metropolitan area, obstructing access to them. The Supreme Court reversed lower court decisions that these protesters had violated federal law by conspiring to deprive women of their constitutional rights to abortion. The law at issue could only be violated by *government* action, not private protesters. Moreover, expressing opposition to abortion is not equivalent to the invidious racial discrimination prohibited by civil rights statutes.[7]

A year later (1994), the Supreme Court considered an assortment of Florida restrictions imposed by court order on pro-life protests outside an abortion clinic. The Court upheld a thirty-six foot "buffer" zone around the clinic entrance and reasonable noise restrictions near the facility. However, it struck down several other limits that were too broad:

- a thirty-six foot buffer zone at the back and sides of the clinic;
- showing images observable by women inside the clinic;
- a restriction on approaching any client within three hundred feet of the clinic; and
- a prohibition on picketing within three hundred feet of a clinic staff member's residence.

Justices Scalia, Kennedy, and Thomas would have struck down all the restrictions because none of the protesters had broken the law, and the restrictions could be used to allow an individual judge to suppress particular (pro-life) ideas.[8]

In 1997, the Court heard a case filed by doctors and abortion clinics against fifty individuals and three organizations that had demonstrated near the clinics and blocked the entrances. A lower federal court banned demonstrations within fifteen feet of the clinics and within fifteen feet of persons entering or leaving them, but allowed sidewalk counselors to engage in "nonthreatening" conversation unless asked to stop. The fifteen-foot ban around the clinics was held constitutional because it ensured public safety, but the floating buffer zone was invalid. It would be difficult to determine compliance—or even to carry on a normal conversation or hand out leaflets at this distance.[9]

## Equal Access to the Campus: Good News for Good News Clubs

The Federal Equal Access Act guarantees public school students the right to form extracurricular groups for religious, philosophical, and political purposes. If a school opens the door for non-curriculum groups to meet during after-school hours, it cannot selectively deny access based on the viewpoint of a particular group.[10] This is good news for Christian students.

Child Evangelism Fellowship is a well-established ministry bringing the gospel to children across America. One of its regular activities is hosting Good News Clubs for kids aged six to twelve. The children sing, pray, read the Bible, and memorize verses. Milford Central School in New York opened its facilities after school hours for community activities, but it denied an application to use school property for a Good News Club because its activities were tantamount to religious worship. The Supreme Court ruled in favor of the Good News Club. The school, having opened its premises, could not discriminate against the Club because of its religious viewpoint. The club meetings were held after school hours, not sponsored by the school, and were voluntary.[11] This decision is *good news* for Christians attending public schools, and it follows the "equal access" pattern established by prior cases.

Twenty years before *Milford*, students at the University of Missouri in Kansas City achieved a similar victory. This college opened its facilities to registered student groups but prohibited the use of school property for religious exercises or teaching. College officials informed Cornerstone, a religious student group that they could no longer meet in university buildings. The Supreme Court decision was *good news* for this group, too. The university could not exclude Cornerstone because of its religious nature.[12]

The *good news* continues. New York law prohibited the use of public school premises for religious purposes—period. However, the Center Moriches Union Free School District opened its doors for outside groups to use school property for after-hours meetings. Lamb's Chapel, an evangelical church in the area, was denied permission to use the premises to show a six-part film series about family values and child rearing from a Christian perspective. The Supreme Court struck down the law because it violated the Free Speech Clause, impermissibly discriminating against groups with a religious viewpoint.[13]

Similarly, religious university students successfully challenged the University of Virginia's denial of funding for their student journal, "Wide Awake: A Christian Perspective at the University of Virginia." Again, the college improperly discriminated against their religious editorial viewpoints.[14]

## Speech in Public Schools: T-Shirts and Other Troubles

There may be good news for after-school Good News Clubs, but students still struggle when they dare to speak about their faith during school hours. Even t-shirts can spell trouble for courageous young Christians who are not ashamed of the gospel of Christ (Rom. 1:16). T-shirts and other peaceful, symbolic expressions are protected under the First Amendment, but school officials don't always know or follow the Constitution.

Public school students do not shed their constitutional rights at the classroom door. So long as they are not disruptive, they have the right to speak and express opinions. That includes symbolic speech such as wearing a t-shirt. Back in the late 1960s, the Supreme Court ruled in favor of high school students suspended for wearing black armbands to protest the Vietnam War.[15] Several later decisions have clarified the circumstances where school officials may lawfully restrict student speech. Schools can limit lewd, vulgar, and indecent speech.[16] Educators can exercise limited editorial control over a school newspaper to protect student privacy— deleting details about a student's pregnancy or a parents' divorce.[17] In the most recent case about student speech, the Supreme Court held that a school could limit speech that advocates illegal drug use.[18]

Several decisions in lower federal courts have vindicated Christian students. James Nixon purchased a t-shirt at a Christian camp and wore it to school. The front displayed the words of Jesus in

John 14:6, "I am the Way, the Truth, and the Life." The backside contained statements that homosexuality is a sin, abortion is murder, and Islam is a lie. School officials ordered James to leave the school when he refused to remove his shirt and threatened suspension if he wore it again, even though it caused no disruption or threats of violence. A federal court in Ohio affirmed this student's right to wear the t-shirt. It could not be banned merely because others found its message offensive.[19]

A high school in Ann Arbor, Michigan held a Diversity Week including panel discussions about race, religion, and sexual orientation. Betsy Hansen, a senior and member of Pioneers for Christ asked to include a clergyman on the Homosexuality and Religion panel to present the biblical view. Her request was denied and the panel consisted of six adult clergy and religious leaders who condoned homosexuality. A federal court found the school's conduct unconstitutional, and observed that:

> This case presents the ironic, and unfortunate, paradox of a public high school celebrating "diversity" by refusing to permit the presentation to students of an "unwelcomed" viewpoint on the topic of homosexuality and religion, while actively promoting the competing view. This practice of "one-way diversity," unsettling in itself, was rendered still more troubling—both constitutionally and ethically—by the fact that the approved viewpoint was, in one manifestation, presented to students as religious doctrine by six clerics (some in full garb) quoting from religious scripture. In its other manifestation, it resulted in the censorship by school administrators of a student's speech about "what diversity means to me," removing that portion of the speech in which the student described the unapproved viewpoint.[20]

Similarly, when a federal court in Maryland considered recommending revisions to a health education curriculum for eighth and tenth grades, it concluded there were serious concerns about both the Free Speech and Establishment Clauses because the materials offered only one opinion about whether homosexuality is a sin, whether AIDS could be God's judgment on homosexuals, and whether churches that consider homosexuality a sin are theologically correct.[21]

Many school speech cases concern high school students, but the problems have trickled down to elementary schools. Culbertson Elementary School held an All About Me Week for kindergarten students. Donna Busch was invited to visit her son Wesley's classroom and read from his favorite book—the Bible. Donna and Wesley chose several verses from Psalm 118, because they often read from the Psalms together. The school refused to allow this because of the perceived separation of church and state. Unfortunately, both the Federal District Court in Pennsylvania and the Third Circuit Court of Appeals ruled against this young believer, even though other students were permitted to read aloud from books about Hanukkah.[22] In cases where elementary school children are involved, schools and courts seem particularly concerned to shield them from anything that might possibly be construed as religious indoctrination. But, as we saw in Chapter 11, courts don't hesitate to rule against parents who object to pro-homosexual indoctrination of their very young children.

## Silence Outside the Sanctuary: IRS Regs Chill Church Speech

Churches and people of faith hold strong positions on public issues. Religious convictions permeate the fabric of our national life. Pastors, congregants, and churches all have the right not only to worship, but also to apply their faith through active participation in the political process. Current tax regulations effectively chill these basic rights by placing an exhorbitant price on their exercise.

Free speech—the hallmark of freedom in America—is denied to an important segment of our society. Churches and other charities jeopardize their tax-exempt status simply by engaging in the wrong type of speech. Their ability to influence legislation is sharply curtailed, and they're absolutely forbidden to endorse or oppose a candidate for political office. Political speech is at the heart of the First Amendment that protects the free uninhibited discussion of governmental affairs. But charities are speechless unless they go to the extra trouble of forming one or more separately incorporated entities to exercise their constitutional rights.

How did this happen? The Revenue Act of 1934 added the following requirement for tax-exempt status under IRC § 501(c)(3): "no substantial part of the activities of which is carrying on propaganda, or otherwise attempting, to influence legislation." In the case leading to this legislation, the Second Circuit rejected the exemption application of the American Birth Control League, because this organization distributed propaganda to the public and legislators urging the repeal of laws preventing birth control.[23] Just twenty years later (1954), Congress added the absolute prohibition against participation in political campaigns—an unconstitutional gag order that survives to this day. As applied to churches, the restrictions also violate the Free Exercise Clause and are thus doubly offensive to the Constitution.

A small church in New York took considerable heat from the IRS in the early 1990s when it paid for two full-page ads urging Christians to vote against Clinton because of his stand on moral issues. The ad stated that:

> This advertisement was co-sponsored by the Church at Pierce Creek, Daniel J. Little, Senior Pastor, and by churches and concerned Christians nationwide. *Tax-deductible donations for this advertisement gladly accepted.* Make donations to: The Church at Pierce Creek. [mailing address].[24]

This case highlights a key point. The Church at Pierce Creek advertised the tax-deductibility of donations for its ad. Since political contributions are not deductible, this fundraising appeal allowed an end-run around the tax laws. *Deductible* charitable contributions were used to fund *non-deductible* political activities. However, the regulations reach far beyond ensuring compliance with the tax laws. Even if no funds are expended, churches are absolutely precluded from even speaking to endorse/oppose political candidates, and they're severely restricted in attempts to participate in the political process.

Charities allegedly have a way out. They can create separate corporations—one under Internal Revenue Code §501(c)(4) for lobbying and another as a §527 "political action committee" (PAC) for campaign involvement. Nevertheless, the government has no good reason to chill core political speech by erecting such expensive roadblocks. Smaller churches may lack the resources to form and maintain separate corporations in order to exercise their fundamental constitutional rights to speak about the political issues and candidates that impact their most cherished religious beliefs. Current regulations extend even to a pastor preaching in the pulpit. Instead, the government might regulate a church's expenditure of funds without restricting the right to speak where no finances are involved. If expenses are necessary, these could be paid privately without the burden of a separate corporation. The *Branch Ministries* ad, for example, could have been funded directly by private individuals rather than using deductible contributions.

Religious beliefs intersect some of the most pressing political issues of our day, and Christians cannot remain silent in good conscience. Enforcing the IRS regulations entangles the secular courts in parsing the religious speech of pastors in the pulpit, and that is an unconstitutional infringement on both free speech and religion. The tax rules are complex—a trap for the unwary. A full review of the fine points is beyond the scope of this book, but church and ministry leaders should be aware of the issues and seek wise counsel in order to comply with obligations to both God and man.

## Hate Crimes—Hate Speech: *Unequal* Protection under the Law

Congress recently enacted a frightening new law that grants special protection to victims of crimes motivated by sexual orientation or gender identity. The Local Law Enforcement and Hate Crimes Prevention Act of 2009 was originally proposed as the Matthew Shepard Act in 2007. It was reintroduced by Representatives John Conyers (Michigan) and Mark Kirk (Illinois) and passed by the House in April 2009. In July 2009, Senate proponents slipped the hate crimes law into the unrelated Department of Defense Authorization Bill. In October 2009, both houses of Congress passed the final version of the legislation and President Obama signed it into law. This law is patently unconstitutional because it gives more protection to crime victims who are homosexual or transgender *than to ordinary victims*. It also erodes the constitutional rights of criminal defendants, punishing them for their alleged *thoughts*. Murder and other violent crimes are already illegal and carry stiff penalties. This hateful law promotes a political agenda by creating specially protected classes based on sexual conduct. It is also alarming because of the potential intrusion on religious freedom and speech—even from the pulpit. It will be extraordinarily difficult for courts to interpret and apply the provisions that punish speech— even though the new law includes an amendment, submitted by Senator Sam Brownback, limiting its reach to speech that incites imminent violence. Several years ago, Swedish pastor Ake Green was convicted of a hate crime and sentenced to a month in jail for preaching against homosexuality. His conviction was overturned on appeal.[25] A Protestant minister in Canada was fined by the Saskatchewan Human Rights Board of Inquiry because he distributed bumper sticks with Bible verses denouncing homosexuality as sin. The Canadian appellate court—unlike its Swedish counterpart— upheld the fine over the pastor's free speech claim.[26] Incidents like this *should not* ever happen in America, but in light of the new hate crimes law—they could.

With the advent of this hate crimes legislation, federal law now codifies disdain for the biblical view of homosexuality. That trend ripples through court cases, state and local laws, the workplace (Chapter 12), and public discourse, shoving Christians to the fringes of our culture and forcing them into litigation to preserve basic liberties that have been taken for granted for decades. Carrie Prejean, Miss California and runner-up for Miss USA 2009, took considerable heat for a simple statement that she did not support same-sex marriage. This young woman lost her title and now supports the National Organization for Marriage.[27]

Kristopher Okwedy, a Staten Island pastor, posted billboards with several translations of a verse condemning homosexuality (Leviticus 18:22). The billboards were displayed in a neighborhood

with many homosexual residents. After several days of public controversy, the Borough President of Staten Island directed
PNE Media—the company that produced and displayed the billboards—to take them down. A federal district court threw out the
pastor's subsequent lawsuit. The Second Circuit Court of Appeals
partially reversed, agreeing that his religious liberty claims should
be dismissed but allowing his free speech claim to go forward.[28]

Canyon Ferry Baptist Church, a small congregation in Montana, collected signatures and hosted a film to encourage support for a pro-marriage amendment to the state constitution. The
church expended a nominal amount for a few photocopies and the
use of its facilities but was called on the carpet by the state Commission of Political Practices for violating Montana's campaign
finance laws. The church was victorious in the Ninth Circuit Court
of Appeals, which found that some of the laws were impermissibly
vague and the church should not have been deemed an "incidental political committee."[29] However, this small congregation had to
wade through more than one courtroom in order to avoid harsh
repercussions for its defense of marriage.

## Speech Wars: Return of the *Unfair* Fairness Doctrine?

The Fairness Doctrine is a Federal Communications Commission
(FCC) rule from the 1940s that was abandoned in 1987. Nevertheless, there are rumors it could make a comeback. Legislation
was introduced in 2005 that would have resurrected the rule,
as it existed in 1987.[30] In 2009, Rep. Maurice Hinchey (D–NY)
announced plans to bring back the 2005 proposal under the name
Media Ownership Reform Act.[31] This *unfair* rule would require
broadcasters to provide opportunities for discussion of conflicting views on important public issues. Such government-mandated
speech is unconstitutional. It may sound good at first, since biblical
views are increasingly marginalized, but a *Christian* radio show host
could be required to grant equal time for pro-abortion and gay-
rights rhetoric. Alternative legislation, the Broadcaster Freedom Act
of 2009, has been introduced in Congress to prevent the resurrection of the "fairness doctrine."[32]

## Seasoned With Salt

In the beginning, God *spoke*. He said "let there be light," and there was light (Gen. 1:3). Unlike any other living creature, human beings are able to speak. Speech is one aspect of our creation in the image of God.

Christians are faced with monumental challenges to speak boldly about the moral issues of our day, and the First Amendment protects their right to do so. In fact, the First Amendment casts a wide protective net over speech, covering everything from blasphemies to blessings.

Scripture is saturated with exhortations about speech. The tongue is a small but powerful part of the body, able to produce praises and curses (James 3:3–12). James cautions readers to be quick to hear, but slow to speak, because human anger does not bring about the righteousness of God (James 1:19–20). There is a time to speak, but also a time to be silent (Eccles. 3:7). Speech should build others up according to their needs (Eph. 4:29). Gentleness characterizes godly speech, in response to anger generally (Prov. 15:1) and before rulers (Prov. 22:11; Prov. 25:15). However, believers are not to be timid about their faith, even in front of a king (Ps. 119:46), speaking truthfully in the power of God (2 Cor. 6:7).

In light of all that God has to say about speech, it's worth asking ourselves a few questions before speaking in the public square and pursuing our First Amendment rights in court. Will our speech advance the mission of the gospel or merely enrage opponents? Does it advance the gospel of Christ to post an isolated verse condemning homosexuality in the workplace, where co-workers will see it and complain without hearing the hope of the gospel? In the *Hewlett Packard* case (Chapter 12), the court commented:

> [W]e will assume *arguendo* that Peterson could establish a prima facie case that his posting of the anti-gay scriptural passages stemmed from his religious beliefs that homosexual activities "violate the commandments of God contained in the Holy Bible" and that those same religious beliefs imposed upon him "a duty to expose evil when confronted with sin." *We make that assumption with considerable reservations,*

*however, because we seriously doubt that the doctrines to which Peterson professes allegiance compel any employee to engage in either expressive or physical activity designed to hurt or harass one's fellow employees.*[33]

Is a Christian employee biblically *required* to post anti-homosexual verses in his workspace? Are there other ways to speak the truth—without compromise—that would better serve the cause of Christ and communicate His gospel? In today's political climate, wisdom is needed to choose legal battles carefully—to advance and not hinder the mission of the gospel.

# Fifteen

# What's Left of
# Religious Rights?

*But even if you should suffer for the sake of righteousness, you are
blessed. And do not fear their intimidation, and do not be troubled, but sanctify Christ as Lord in your hearts, always ready to
make a defense to everyone who asks you to give an account for
the hope that is in you, yet with gentleness and reverence; and
keep a good conscience so that in the thing in which you are slan-
dered, those who revile your good behavior in Christ may be put
to shame* (1 PETER 3:14–16 NASB).

*For the Lord is our judge, the Lord is our lawgiver, the Lord is our
king; He will save us* (ISAIAH 33:22 ESV).

Where do we go from here? There is much more at
stake than the right to be left alone to operate ministries and
businesses according to biblical principles. Perhaps, if courts don't
allow activists to shred our Constitution, Christian doctors can opt
out of performing abortions or fertilizing lesbians. However, babies
may still be slaughtered or ushered into a perverted parallel universe where women marry women and men sleep with men. This
is unacceptable. If it continues, our formerly Christian nation will

one day be dead and buried, and God will no longer bless America. Believers must be equipped with information and spiritual wisdom so they will be able to take action where possible and hold firmly to their faith if faced with litigation—or even persecution.

We are unquestionably in a spiritual battle of major proportions. We wrestle not against flesh and blood—the homosexual, the abortionists, and others who desperately need the gospel, but against spiritual powers of wickedness in the heavenly places (Eph. 6:10–20). Believers are citizens of heaven (Phil. 3:20; Col. 3:1–3) who will one day inherit the earth (Matt. 5:5). But not yet.

## One Nation . . . Six Feet Under?

The foundation is already crumbling. Shortly after his inauguration, President Barack Obama attended a press conference in Turkey and announced that in spite of America's large Christian population: "[W]e do not consider ourselves a Christian nation or a Jewish nation or a Muslim nation; we consider ourselves a nation of citizens who are bound by ideals and a set of values."[1]

After the prophet Elijah victoriously confronted the prophets of Baal, he complained to the Lord that the Israelites had rejected His covenant, broken down His altars, killed His prophets, and Elijah's own life was now in danger (1 Kings 19:10). Elijah thought he was the only faithful one left, but God assured Him that He had reserved *seven thousand* who had not bowed down to Baal (1 Kings 19:18). America may not be the Christian nation it once was, but there are still many faithful believers, not only in this country but also throughout the world. God's kingdom is alive and well. He will build His church, and the gates of hell cannot prevail against it (Matt. 16:18).

However, until that kingdom is fully consummated, we face the trials and tribulations of living in a sinful world. Believers need to be alert and informed, take action where possible, and if challenged by litigation, hold firmly to the faith once and for all delivered to the saints (Jude 3).

## Wake Up and Watch

Centuries ago, the Lord told Ezekiel that He was appointing him as a watchman for Israel (Ezek. 3:17). Many watchmen are needed in America today.

As this chapter is written, an e-mail alert has come in from Advocates for Faith and Freedom. California legislators have introduced Senate Bill 572 to require the Governor to declare May 22 of each year Harvey Milk Day to honor the life and political career of homosexual activist Harvey Milk. The bill would also encourage public schools to conduct commemorative exercises promoting the homosexual agenda—even to kindergarten children.[2] Meanwhile, Alliance Defense Fund reported the good news that a federal court had bounced a gay couple's challenge to the California Supreme Court decision to uphold the state constitutional marriage amendment enacted by voters in the fall of 2008 (Proposition 8).[3] But the good news was short-lived, as marriage went on trial in San Francisco at the U.S. District Court for the Northern District of California. The trial concluded on January 27, 2010.[4] Perhaps this battle will reach the U.S. Supreme Court.

There is a wealth of information available online, in addition to radio, television, newspapers, magazines, and other media. (Sometimes it can be overwhelming!) Organizations like Alliance Defense Fund, American Center for Law and Justice, Advocates for Faith and Freedom, Pacific Justice Institute—plus many other national and local groups—offer free e-mail alerts to help believers stay informed about the pressing moral/political issues of our day. The Resources at the back provide a list of websites and organizations involved in the battle for religious liberty. It can also be helpful to browse the sites of opponents such as the ACLU and Lamba Legal to understand their strategy. When election time rolls around, Christians can learn about their candidates—their past voting records and positions. Websites sometimes disclose names of organizations that endorse a particular candidate. Checking out those endorsements may reveal more about how the candidate will perform if elected. Christians are best equipped to take action and make a difference if they're informed.

The political scene changes daily. New cases are filed and laws enacted. This book must go to press at some point, and by the time you read these words, there will be new developments—new court cases and new laws that expand or restrict religious liberty. Hopefully you will have some new tools to keep abreast of those changes and challenges as they happen.

## Get Up and Go

Not everyone can do everything—but everyone can do *something*. While I was working on this manuscript one weekend, some of my pro-life friends were hosting a table for the North Carolina Right to Life at a local shrimp festival. We can all pray. Some are able to donate funds. Others can give their time and talents. Crisis pregnancy centers need volunteers to give practical help and counsel to young women, facilitating alternatives to abortion. There is a myriad of opportunities.

Those opportunities begin at home. If you are a parent, knowing your child's school curriculum and policies will help you protect your child from spiritual harm. A recent e-mail alert from Pacific Justice Institute warned readers that the School Board in Modesto, California was considering a policy to allow students to leave campus for confidential medical services—such as abortions—without notice to parents.[5] Concerned parents who know about such a proposal can speak up and object.

One vote may not seem important, but many votes and voices can make a difference. America is still a democracy with elected representatives responsible to those who placed them in office. Many informative e-mail alerts allow readers to access online petitions and information about how to contact their federal, state, and local legislators by phone, letter, FAX, or e-mail.

## Fight the Good Fight

As the Apostle Paul's earthly life drew to a close, he declared that he had "fought the good fight" and finished the race (2 Tim. 4:7). He encouraged Timothy to fight that same "good fight" (1 Tim.

1:18, 6:12). Today we continue the "good fight" to advance the ministry of the gospel that Jesus Christ entrusted to us. Occasionally we are called to fight that battle in the courtrooms of America, to protect our freedom to preach the gospel and live according to God's Word in the public square. Believers are blessed with organizations and Christian lawyers who give sacrificially of their time, treasures, and talents to defend and prosecute those legal actions when necessary.

The ancient Israelites experienced an amazing victory during King Jehoshaphat's reign (2 Chr. 20:1–29). Faced with a vast army of Moabites, Ammonites, and a few Meunites, the alarmed King of Judah proclaimed a fast and called an assembly to seek the Lord. After his passionate public prayer acknowledging God's sovereign power, Jahaziel was filled with the Holy Spirit and brought some incredible words of hope. The people were to go out and face the enemy, stand firm, and watch the Lord deliver them. They headed for battle singing and praising God: "Give thanks to the Lord, for His love endures forever" (2 Chr. 20:21). The Lord kept His promise and gave them victory over the enemies who had planned to annihilate them.

Our victory will not look exactly like this one, but we worship and serve the same Lord who delivered His people in King Jehoshaphat's day. There is a seemingly vast army aligned against Christianity in America. However, America is one piece of a much larger puzzle. There have been forces aligned against God's kingdom throughout the ages, and so it will be until the Lord returns to gather His people and usher in His kingdom that will never end. Nevertheless, we have the Book, and we know how the story will end. As the Hallelujah Chorus in Handel's Messiah proclaims, *"He shall reign forever and ever."*

# Resources

Advocates for Faith and
   Freedom
www.faith-freedom.com

Advocates International
www.advocatesinternational.org

Alliance Defense Fund
www.alliancedefensefund.org

American Center for Law and
   Justice (ACLJ)
www.aclj.org

Americans United for Life
www.aul.org

Bioethics Defense Fund
www.bdfund.org

Christian Law Association
www.christianlaw.org

Christian Legal Society
www.clsnet.org

Family Research Council
www.frc.org

Family Research Institute
www.familyresearchinst.org

Foundation for Moral Law
www.morallaw.org/

Gateways to Better Education
www.gtbe.org

The Heritage Foundation
www.MyHeritage.org

Justice and Freedom Fund
www.justiceandfreedom.org

Liberty Counsel
www.lc.org

Life Training Institute
www.prolifetraining.com

National Council on Bible Curriculum in Public Schools
www.bibleinschools.net

National Organization for Marriage
www.nationformarriage.org.

The National Legal Foundation
www.nlf.net

National Right to Life
www.nrlc.org

North American Religious Liberty Association
www.churchstate.org

North Carolina Family Policy Council
www.ncfamily.org

Pacific Justice Institute
www.pacificjustice.org

Parents and Friends of Ex-Gays & Gays (PFOX)
www.pfox.org

Peacemaker Ministries
www.peacemaker.net

PersonhoodUSA
www.personhoodusa.com

Reclaim America
www.reclaimamerica.org

Regent Law School
www.regent.edu

Return America (North Carolina)
www.returnamerica.org

The Rutherford Institute
www.rutherford.org

Wallbuilders
www.wallbuilders.com

# Endnotes

## Introduction

1. An amicus ("friend of the court") brief is filed by someone who is not a party to the case but has an interest in the outcome. Sometimes organizations file such briefs to assist the court in making the right decision.

## Chapter 1

1. *Startzell v. City of Philadelphia* (3d. Cir. 2008) 533 F.3d 183.

2. David Barton, *Original Intent: The Courts, the Constitution, and Religion* (Aledo, TX: Wallbuilders, 2005), p. 46, n. 14, citing Thomas Jefferson, *Notes on the States of Virginia* (Philadelphia: Mathew Carey, 1794), p. 237, Query XVIII.

3. David Barton, *Original Intent*, p. 111, n. 143, citing James Madison, *The Papers of James Madison*, Henry Gilpin, ed. (Washington: Langtree and O'Sullivan, 1840), Vol. II, p. 984–986, June 28, 1787.

4. David Barton, *Original Intent*, p. 319, n. 2, citing John Adams, *The Works of John Adams, Second President of the United States*, Charles Francis Adams, ed. (Boston: Little, Brown, 1854), Vol. IX, p. 229, October 11, 1798.

5. *Updegraph v. The Commonwealth* (Penn. 1824) 11 Serg. & Rawle 394, 400.

6. *Church of the Holy Trinity v. United States* (1892) 143 U.S. 457, 465.

7. *Ibid.* at 471.

8. *United States v. Macintosh* (1931) 283 U.S. 605, 625 (italics in original; bold emphasis added).

## Chapter 2

1. *Constance J. Rehm v. Rolling Hills Consolidated Library and Patricia Lamb*, in the United States District Court for the Western District of Missouri, St. Joseph Division *(2004)*.

2. www.ffrf.org.

3. www.aclu.org.

4. www.au.org.

5. www.pfaw.org.

6. David Barton, *Original Intent: The Courts, the Constitution, and Religion* (Aledo, TX: Wallbuilders, 2005), p. 45–46, n. 12, citing Thomas Jefferson, *Writings of Thomas Jefferson*, Albert Ellery Bergh, ed. (Washington, D.C.: The Thomas Jefferson Memorial Association, 1904), Vol. XVI, pp. 281–282, to the Danbury Baptist Association on January 1, 1802 (emphasis added).

7. *Reynolds v. United States* (1878) 98 U.S. 145.

8. *Everson v. Board of Education* (1947) 330 U.S. 1.

9. *Ibid.* at 12–13.

10. *Ibid.* at 18.

11. *McCollum v. Board of Education*, 333 U.S. 203, 256 (1948).

12. *Zorach v. Clauson*, 343 U.S. 306, 312–313 (1952).

13. *Flast v. Cohen* (1968) 392 U.S. 83.

14. *Lemon v. Kurtzman*, 403 U.S. 602 (1971).

15. *Witters v. Washington Dept. of Services for the Blind* (1986) 474 U.S. 481.

16. *Zobrest v. Catalina Foothills School District* (1993) 509 U.S. 1.

17. *Agostini v. Felton* (1997) 521 U.S. 203.

18. *Zelman v. Simmons-Harris* (2002) 536 U.S. 639.

19. *Bowen v. Kendrick* (1988) 487 U.S. 589.

20. *Tilton v. Richardson* (1971) 403 U.S. 672.

21. *Roemer v. Board of Public Works* (1976) 426 U.S. 736.

22. *Marsh v. Chambers* (1983) 463 U.S. 783.

23. *Elk Grove Unified Sch. Dist. v. Newdow*, 542 U.S. 1 (2004).

24. C.F., et al., v. Capistrano Unified School District, et al., Case No. SACV 07–1434 JVS (ANx) in the United States District Court, Central District of California (2009).

25. *U. S. v. Ballard* (1944) 322 U.S. 78.

26. *Torcaso v. Watkins* (1961) 367 U.S. 488.

27. *McDaniel v. Paty* (1978) 435 U.S. 618.

28. *Sherbert v. Verner* (1963) 374 U.S. 398.

29. *Thomas v. Review Bd. of Ind. Employment Sec. Div.* (1981) 450 U.S. 707.

30. *Hobbie v. Unemployment Appeals Comm.* (1987) 480 U.S. 136.

31. *Frazee v. Illinois Dept. of Employment Sec.* (1989) 489 U.S. 829.

32. *United States v. Lee* (1982) 455 U.S. 252.

33. *Trans World Airlines v. Hardison* (1977) 432 U.S. 63.

34. *Goldman v. Weinberger* (1986) 475 U.S. 503; *O'Lone v. Estate of Shabazz* (1987) 482 U.S. 342.

35. *Bowen v. Roy* (1986) (1986) 476 U.S. 693.

36. *Lyng v. Northwest Indian Cemetery Protective Ass'n* (1988) 485 U.S. 439.

## Chapter 3

1. *North Coast Women's Medical Care, Inc. v. Benitez* (2008) 44 Cal.4th 1145 ("*Benitez*").

2. *Employment Div. v. Smith* (1990) 494 U.S. 872 ("*Smith*").

3. *Reynolds v. United States* (1878) 98 U.S. 145, 163 ("*Reynolds*").

4. *Ibid.* at 166.

5. *Davis v. Beason* (1890) 133 U.S. 333 ("*Davis*").

6. *Ibid.* at 342.

7. *Smith* at 885 (emphasis added).

8. *Reynolds; Davis.*

9. *Prince v. Massachusetts* (1944) 321 U.S. 158.

10. *Braunfeld v. Brown* (1962) 366 U.S. 599.

11. *United States v. Lee* (1982) 455 U.S. 252.

12. *Church of Lukumi Babalu Aye v. City of Hialeah* (1993) 508 U.S. 520.

13. *Smith* at 881.

14. *Pierce v. Society of Sisters* (1925) 268 U.S. 510.

15. *Wisconsin v. Yoder* (1972) 406 U.S. 205 ("*Yoder*").

16. *West Virginia Bd. of Education v. Barnette* (1943) 319 U.S. 624.

17. Michael W. McConnell, *God is Dead and We Have Killed Him! Freedom of Religion in the Post-Modern Age,* 1993 BYU L. Rev. 163, 172–174.

18. *Yoder.*

19. *Smith* at 908.

20. *Smith v. Fair Employment and Housing Commission* (1996) 12 Cal.4th 1143, 1196, 1227; Gerard V. Bradley, *Beguiled: Free Exercise Exemptions And The Siren Song of Liberalism,* 20 Hofstra L. Rev. 245, 246 (1991).

21. *Smith* at 899–900.

22. 42 U.S.C. § 2000bb(a).

23. *Sherbert v. Verner* (1963) 374 U.S. 398; *Yoder.*

24. 42 U.S.C. § 2000bb(b).

25. *Church of Lukumi Babalu Aye, Inc. v. City of Hialeah* (1993) 508 U.S. 520, 562, 564.

26. *City of Boerne v. Flores* (1997) 521 U.S. 507 ("*City of Boerne*").

27. *Gonzales v. O Centro Espirita Beneficente* (2006) 546 U.S. 418.

28. 42 U.S.C.S. § 2000cc et seq.

29. *Cutter v. Wilkinson* (2005) 544 U.S. 709.

30. *Bob Jones Univ. v. United States* (1983) 461 U.S. 574.

31. *Benitez* at 1158.

32. Richard F. Duncan, *Who Wants to Stop the Church: Homosexual Rights Legislation, Public Policy, and Religious Freedom,* 69 Notre Dame L. Rev. 393, 420 (1994); Douglas Laycock, *The Remnants of Free Exercise,* 1990 Sup. Ct. Rev. 1, 4.

33. *City of Boerne;* Teresa S. Collett, *Heads, Secularists Win; Tails, Believers Lose—Returning Only Free Exercise to the Political Process,* 20 U. Ark. Little Rock L.J. 689, 693–695 (1998).

## Chapter 4

1. *Rosenbaum v. City and County of San Francisco* (9th Cir. 2007) 484 F.3d 1142.

2. *Smith v. Fair Employment and Housing Commission* (1996) 12 Cal.4th 1143, 1155 ("*Smith v. FEHC*"); citing *Swanner v. Anchorage Equal Rights Commission* (Alaska 1994) 874 P.2d 274, 278, fn. 4.

3. *Smith v. FEHC* at 1161–62.

4. *Braunfled v. Brown* (1961) 366 U.S. 599, 605 (Jewish merchants lost a challenge to Sunday closing laws, which effectively required them to close their businesses on both Saturday and Sunday).

5. *Smith v. FEHC* at 1170.

6. *Ibid.* at 656–657.

7. *Boy Scouts v. Dale* (2000) 530 U.S. 640, 650.

8. *Ibid.* at 648.

9. *Ibid.* at 653. . . The Jaycees and Rotary lost free association claims because they could not show that their organizational expression was actually hindered by admitting female members. *Roberts v. United States Jaycees* (1984) 468 U.S. 609, 624; *Board of Directors of Rotary International v. Rotary Club of Duarte* (1987) 481 U.S. 537, 548.

10. *Boy Scouts of Am. v. Wyman* (2d Cir. 2003) 335 F.3d 80, 94.

11. *Christian Legal Society v. Walker* (7th Cir. 2006) 453 F.3d 853, 863.

12. *Ibid.* at 863.

13. The U.S. Supreme Court granted review of this case in December 2009, and oral argument is scheduled in April 2010.

14. *R.A.V. v. City of St. Paul* (1992) 505 U.S. 377, 390.

15. *Christian Legal Society v. Kane* (N.D. Cal. 2006) 2006 U.S. Dist. LEXIS 27347.

16. See, e.g., Eph. 5:22–33; 1 Tim. 2:9–15, 3:1–13.

17. *Catholic Charities of Sacramento, Inc. v. Superior Court* (2004) 32 Cal.4th 527, 550.

18. *Ibid.* at 564.

19. *Ibid.* at 565 (Brown, J., dissenting).

20. *Ibid.* at 565.

## Chapter 5

1. "In one week, four ADF lawsuits compel four schools to allow pro-life student speech on Roe v. Wade," January 22, 2007, available at www.alliancedefensefund.org/news/pressrelease.aspx?cid=3988 (last visited July 30, 2009).

2. Senate Bill 1173 and House of Representatives Bill 1964.

3. See www.nrlc.org/FOCA for current updates on this legislation.

4. *Gonzales v. Carhart* (2007) 550 U.S. 124 ("*Gonzales v. Carhart*").

5. *Griswold v. Connecticut* (1965) 381 U.S. 479.

6. *Eisenstadt v. Baird* (1972) 405 U.S. 438.

7. *Ibid.* at 453.

8. *U.S. v. Vuitch* (1971) 402 U.S. 62.

9. *Roe v. Wade* (1973) 410 U.S. 113 ("*Roe*").

10. *Doe v. Bolton* (1973) 410 U.S. 179.

11. *Ibid.* at 214.

12. *Roe* at 159.

13. *Ibid.* at 129–141.

14. *Ibid.* at 154; *Jacobson v. Massachusetts* (1905) 197 U.S. 11.

15. *Roe* at 158.

16. *Ibid.* at 153.

17. *Ibid.* at 157, n. 54.

18. *Planned Parenthood of Southeastern Pennsylvania v. Casey* (1992) 505 U.S. 833 ("*Casey*").

19. *Ibid.* at 846.

20. *Ibid.* at 850.

21. *Ibid.* at 851.

22. *Ibid.* at 851.

23. *Ibid.* at 877.

24. *Singleton v. Wulff* (1976) 428 U.S. 106.

25. *Roe* at 160.

26. *Planned Parenthood v. Danforth* (1976) 428 U.S. 52 (*"PP v. Danforth"*).

27. *Colautti v. Franklin* (1979) 439 U.S. 379.

28. *Anders v. Floyd* (1979) 440 U.S. 445.

29. *Webster v. Repro Health* (1989) 492 U.S. 490.

30. *Casey* at 990, n. 5 (Scalia, J., dissenting).

31. *PP v. Danforth*.

32. *City of Akron v. Akron Center* (1983) 462 U.S. 416 (*"Akron I"*).

33. *Thornburgh v. Am College* (1986) 476 U.S. 747, 762 (*"Thornburgh"*); quoting *Akron I* at 443–444.

34. *Casey* at 882.

35. *Gonzales v. Carhart* at 159.

36. *Ibid.* at 159–160.

37. *PP v. Danforth*.

38. *Bellotti v. Baird I* (1976) 428 U.S. 132; *Bellotti v. Baird II* (1979) 443 U.S. 622.

39. *H.L. v. Matheson* (1981) 450 U.S. 398.

40. *Akron I*.

41. *Planned Parenthood v. Ashcroft* (1983) 462 U.S. 476.

42. *Hodgson v. MN* (1990) 497 U.S. 417.

43. *Ohio v. Akron Center for Reproductive Health* (1990) 497 U.S. 502 (*"Akron II"*).

44. *Casey*.

45. *Lambert v. Wicklund* (1997) 520 U.S. 292.

46. *PP v. Danforth*.

47. *Doe v. Smith* (1988) 486 U.S. 1308.

48. *Casey* at 974.

49. *Ibid.* at 893–894.

50. *Ibid.* at 896–897.

51. *Connecticut v. Menillo* (1975) 423 U.S. 9.

52. *Mazurek v. Armstrong* (1997) 520 U.S. 968.

53. *Thornburgh*.

54. *Akron I*.

55. *Planned Parenthood v. Ashcroft* (1983) 462 U.S. 476.

56. *Simopoulos v. Virginia* (1983) 462 U.S. 506.

57. *Maher v. Roe* (1977) 432 U.S. 464 (a Connection Welfare Department regulation limited Medicaid abortion benefit during the first trimester to those medically necessary); *Beal v. Doe* (1977) 432 U.S. 438 (Pennsylvania law restricted Medicaid abortion assistance to cases involving threats to health, rape/incest, or babies with physical deformities).

58. *Harris v. McRae* (1980) 448 U.S. 297; *Williams v. Abaraz* (1980) 448 U.S. 358.

59. *Dalton v. Little Rock* (1996) 516 U.S. 474.

60. *Rust v. Sullivan* (1991) 500 U.S. 173.

61. *Poelker v. Doe* (1977) 432 U.S. 519.

62. *Webster v. Repro Health* (1989) 492 U.S. 490.

63. *Catholic Charities of Sacramento, Inc. v. Superior Court* (2004) 32 Cal.4th 527.

64. *Richmond Med. Ctr. for Women v. Gilmore* (4th Cir 1998) 144 F.3d 326.

65. *Planned Parenthood of Wisconsin v. Doyle* (7th Cir 1998) 162 F.3d 463.

66. *Stenberg v. Carhart* (2000) 530 U.S. 914, 922.

67. *Gonzales v. Carhart.*

68. *Ibid.* at 157 (Congressional Findings (14)(N)).

69. *Ibid.* at 157 (Congressional Findings (14)(J)).

70. *Ibid.* at 158 (Congressional Findings (14)(L)).

71. *Richmond Med Ctr. for Women v. Herring* 2009 U.S. App. LEXIS 13593, 46–47.

72. *Cruzan v. Director* (1990) 497 U.S. 261.

73. David Gibbs, *Fighting for Dear Life* (Minneapolis, MN: Bethany House, 2006). This book is an excellent behind-the-scenes account written by the attorney who represented Terry Schiavo's parents.

74. *Vacco v. Quill* (1997) 521 U.S. 793.

75. For additional information, see www.personhoodusa.com.

## Chapter 6

1. Walter J. Walsh, *The Fearful Symmetry of Gay Rights, Religious Freedom, and Racial Equality*, 40 How. L.J. 513, 546, 570 (1997).

2. William N. Eskridge, Jr., *A Jurisprudence of "Coming Out": Religion, Homosexuality, Collisions of Liberty and Equality in American Public Law*, 106 Yale L.J. 2411, 2473 (1997).

3. *United States v. Ballard* (1944) 322 U.S. 78, 95.

4. David E. Bernstein, *Defending the First Amendment From Antidiscrimination*, 82 N.C. L. Rev. 223, 245 (2003).

5. SEN.REP. No. 103–111, 1st Sess., at 4 (1993), *reprinted in* 1993 U.S.C.C.A.N., 1893–1894; cited by Kennard, J., dissenting, in *Smith v. Fair Employment and Housing Commission* (1996) 12 Cal.4th 1143, 1192.

6. *Girouard v. United States* (1946) 328 U.S. 61, 68.

7. *Gay Rights Coalition of Georgetown Univ. Law Ctr. v. Georgetown Univ.* (D.C. 1987) 536 A.2d 1 (en banc).

8. *Christian Legal Society v. Walker* (7th Cir. 2006) 453 F.3d 853, 863.

9. *Planned Parenthood of Southeastern Pennsylvania v. Casey* (1992) 505 U.S. 833, 982 (Scalia, J., dissenting) ("*Casey*").

10. *Roe v. Wade* (1973) 410 U.S. 113, 157 ("*Roe*").

11. *Roe* at 169–170 (emphasis added); this statement is quoted in the 1992 *Casey* decision affirming *Roe*. *Casey* at 851.

12. *Abele v. Markle* (Conn. 1972) 351 F. Supp. 224, 227 (emphasis added), quoted in *Roe* at 170 (Stewart, J., concurring).

13. *Doe v. Bolton* (1973) 410 U.S. 179, 214–215 (emphasis added).

14. *Casey* at 852 (emphasis added).

15. *Casey* at 877.

16. *Ibid.* at 852 (emphasis added).

17. Emily Bazelon, "The Place of Women on the Court," *New York Times*, July 5, 2009, available at http://www.nytimes.com/2009/07/12/magazine/12ginsburg-t.html?scp=3&sq=emily%20bazelon&st=cse (last visited August 18, 2009).

18. *Gonzales v. Carhart* (2007) 550 U.S. 124, 197 (Ginsburg, J., dissenting).

19. *Ibid.* at 191 (Ginsburg, J., dissenting) (emphasis added).

20. "SLED" was coined by Dr. Stephen D. Schwartz, *The Moral Question of Abortion*, (Chicago: Loyola University Press, 1990), pp. 15–18, and popularized by

Scott Klusendorf, President of Life Training Institute. See http://prolifetraining.
com/Articles/FiveMinute1.htm.
21. *Casey* at 856 (emphasis added).
22. *Casey* at 859.
23. *Wooley v. Maynard* (1977) 430 U.S. 705.
24. *Washington v. Glucksberg* (1997) 521 U.S. 702, 782–786 (Souter, J.,
concurring).
25. *Casey* at 980 (Scalia, J., dissenting).
26. *Ibid.* at 867.
27. *Ibid.* at 885.
28. *Brown v. Board of Education* (1955) 349 U.S. 294.
29. *Plessy v. Ferguson* (1896) 163 U.S. 537.
30. *West Coast Hotel Co. v. Parrish* (1937) 300 U.S. 379.
31. *Lochner v. New York* (1905) 198 U.S. 45 (holding that state could not limit
working hours in a bakery); *Adkins v. Children's Hospital of District of Columbia*
(1923) 261 U.S. 525 (holding that state could not impose minimum wage requirements for adult women employees).
32. *Lawrence v. Texas* (2003) 539 U.S. 558.
33. *Bowers v. Hardwick* (1986) 478 U.S. 186, 197 (Burger, J., concurring).
34. *Casey* at 984 (Scalia, J., dissenting).

## Chapter 7

1. See http://www.lambdalegal.org/in-court/cases/in-the-matter-of-brian.
html. The case is *In the Matter of Brian (A.K.A. Mariah)*. It was opened on April
14, 2006 and closed on September 4, 2008.
2. California, Connecticut, District of Columbia, Illinois, Indiana, Maine,
Massachusetts, Nevada (some jurisdictions), New Hampshire (some jurisdictions),
New Jersey, New York, Oregon, and Vermont. Some states allow a same-sex co-
partner to adopt the partner's child: California, Colorado, Connecticut, District of
Columbia, Illinois, Louisiana, Massachusetts, New Jersey, New York, Pennsylvania,
and Vermont.
3. Alabama, Alaska, Delaware, Hawaii, Iowa, Louisiana, Maryland, Minne-
sota, Nevada, New Hampshire, New Mexico, Oregon, Rhode Island, Texas, and
Washington.
4. Alabama, Alaska, Arizona, Arkansas, Colorado, Delaware, District of Columbia, Georgia, Hawaii, Idaho, Indiana, Iowa, Kansas, Kentucky, Louisiana, Maine,
Maryland, Massachusetts, Michigan, Minnesota, Mississippi, Missouri, Montana,
Nebraska, Nevada, New Hampshire, New Jersey, New Mexico, New York, North
Carolina, North Dakota, Ohio, Oklahoma, Oregon, Pennsylvania, Rhode Island,
South Carolina, South Dakota, Tennessee, Texas, Utah, Vermont, Virginia, Washington, West Virginia, Wisconsin, and Wyoming.
5. The information in this paragraph was compiled from the website of the
Human Rights Campaign (www.hrc.org), one of many pro-homosexual advocacy
groups. The site was last reviewed on July 14, 2009 and indicated that it was last
updated on July 9, 2009.
6. Public Law No. 111-84.
7. H.R. 3017, co-sponsored in the U.S. House of Representatives by Repre-
sentive Barney Frank (Democrat from Massachusetts) and Ileana Ros-Lehtinen
(Republican from Florida), with a total of 117 original co-sponsors.

8. For more details and updated information, see: http://www.faith-freedom. com/in-the-courts/california-education-committee-v-arnold-schwarzenegger.

9. *Roe v. Wade* (1973) 410 U.S. 113, 132–136, 159–163.

10. *In re Marriage Cases* (2006) 143 Cal.App.4th 873, 938 (Parrilli, J., concurring). The California Supreme Court granted review and reversed, finding a constitutional right to same-sex marriage. Voters approved Proposition 8 by a slim margin, amending the state constitution to protect the original definition of marriage. Activists then challenged the constitutional amendment as an improper "revision." The California Supreme Court rejected their legal arguments but validated the same-sex marriages performed in California between the court decision and the passage of Prop 8. Federal courts have rejected additional challenges. But this story is far from over.

11. *Bowers v. Hardwick* (1986) 478 U.S. 186, 197 (Burger, J., concurring) ("*Bowers*"). The U.S. Supreme Court upheld a law in Georgia that prohibited sodomy, holding that there is no "fundamental right" to engage in homosexual sodomy.

12. Richard F. Duncan, *Who Wants to Stop the Church: Homosexual Rights Legislation, Public Policy, and Religious Freedom*, 69 Notre Dame L. Rev. 393, 415 (1994). This article is an excellent warning about the homosexual threat to religious liberty.

13. *Lawrence v. Texas* (2003) 539 U.S. 558, 571 (emphasis added) ("*Lawrence*").

14. Duncan, *Who Wants to Stop the Church*, *supra*, 415.

15. See www.domawatch.org/amendments for a current list.

16. *Romer v. Evans* (1996) 517 U.S. 620 ("*Romer*").

17. *Equality Foundation of Greater Cincinnati v. City of Cincinnati* (6th Cir. 1997) 128 F.3d 289 ("*Equality Fdn.*").

18. *Planned Parenthood v. Casey* (1992) 505 U.S. 833; see Chapter 5.

19. *Rumsfeld v. Forum for Academic and Institutional Rights, Inc.* (2006) 547 U.S. 47.

20. 10 U.S.C. § 983 (the "Solomon Amendment").

21. *Moore v. City of East Cleveland, Ohio* (1977) 431 U.S. 494, 503.

22. *Palko v. Connecticut* (1937) 302 U.S. 319, 325.

23. *Woodward v. U.S.*, (Fed. Cir. 1989) 871 F.2d 1068, 1074; *High Tech Gays v. Defense Industrial Security Clearance Office* (9th Cir. 1990) 895 F.2d 563, 574; *Dahl v. Secretary of the United States Navy* , (E.D. Ca. 1993) 830 F. Supp. 1319, 1324; *Philips v. Perry*, (9th Cir. 1997) 106 F.3d 1420, 1426; *Lofton v. Dept. of Children and Family Svsc.* (11th Cir. 2004) 358 F.3d 804, 815–817; *Cook v. Rumsfeld*, (D. Mass. 2006) 429 F.Supp.2d 385, 396–397.

24. *Washington v. Glucksberg* (1997) 521 U.S. 702, 720–1 (rejecting fundamental right to suicide).

25. *Bowers* at 191.

26. *Lawrence* at 586 (Scalia, J., dissenting, observed that *Bowers'* outcome was overruled but its central legal conclusion left untouched).

27. *Cook v. Rumsfeld*, (D. Mass. 2006) 429 F.Supp.2d 385, 394, n. 10.

28. *Romer* at 626.

29. *Equality Fnd. . .*

30. See, e.g., www.aclu.org/lgbt (American Civil Liberties Union); www.nclrights.org (National Center for Lesbian Rights); www.lambdalegal.org (Lambda Legal); www.now.org (National Organization for Women); www.pflag.org

(Parents, Families, & Friends of Lesbians and Gays); www.glsen.org (Gay, Lesbian, and Straight Education Network); www.hrc.org (Human Rights Campaign). These are just a small sample.

## Chapter 8

1. *Jones v. Barlow* (2007) 154 P.3d 808.

2. *Mason v. Dwinnell* (N.C. Ct. App. 2008) 660 S.E.2d 58.

3. "Amending Birth Certificates to Reflect Your Correct Sex," published November 12, 2002 (document updated October 1, 2007), available online at www.lambdalegal.org/our-work/publications/facts-backgrounds/page–31991108. html (last visited August 20, 2009).

4. Eugene Volokh, *Same-Sex Marriage and Slippery Slopes*, 33 Hofstra L. Rev. 1155, 1178 (2005).

5. S.B. 526 and H.B. 88; "LGBT Advocates Celebrate New Laws," reported by the North Carolina Family Policy Council on July 13, 2009 on its website: http://ncfamily.org/stories/090713s1.html (last visited August 22, 2009).

6. New Business Items Under Consideration at the 2009 Representative Assembly, National Educational Association, available online at www.nea.org/grants/33354.htm (last visited August 20, 2009). See New Business Item "E."

7. *Boy Scouts of Am. v. Wyman* (2d. Cir. 2003) 335 F.3d 80.

8. Ian Urbina, "Boy Scouts Lose Philadelphia Lease in Gay-Rights Fight," *The New York Times*, December 4, 2007, available online at www.nytimes.com/2007/12/06/us/06scouts.html (last visited August 20, 2009).

9. *Evans v. City of Berkeley* (2006) 38 Cal.4th 1.

10. *Bob Jones Univ. v. United States* (1983) 461 U.S. 574 (*Bob Jones University*).

11. *Levin v. Yeshiva Univ.* (N.Y. 2001) 754 N.E.2d 1099.

12. *Goodridge v. Department of Public Health* (Mass. 2003) 798 N.E.2d 941, 954.

13. *Sutton v. Warren* (1845) 51 Mass. 451, 452.

14. *Martin v. Commonwealth* (1805) 1 Mass. 346, 398.

15. *Pratt v. Pratt* (Mass. 1892) 32 N.E. 747, 748.

16. *Thomas v. Review Bd.* (1981) 450 U.S. 707, 713–714. . .

17. *Smith v. Fair Employment and Housing Commission* (1996) 12 Cal.4th 1143, 1182, 1191–92 (inquiry unavoidable); *Gay Rights Coalition of Georgetown Univ. Law Ctr. v. Georgetown Univ.* (D.C. 1987) 536 A.2d 1, 15 (review of Catholic doctrine regarding homosexual sin); *Valov v. Dept. of Motor Vehicles* (2005) 132 Cal.App.4th 1113, 1118 (quotes Exodus 4:20); *Gonzales v. O Centro Espirita Beneficente* (2006) 126 S. Ct. 1211, 1223 (affirming feasibility of case-by-case determination).

18. *Boy Scouts of Am. v. Dale* (2000) 530 U.S. 640, 686–688 ("*Dale*").

19. Jack S. Vaitayanonta, NOTE: *In State Legislatures We Trust? The "Compelling Interest" Presumption and Religious Free Exercise Challenges to State Civil Rights Laws*, 101 Colum. L. Rev. 886, 923 (2001). This commentator recommends that, in religious challenges to anti-discrimination laws, courts presuppose that the government has a "compelling interest" in enforcement of the law.

20. Peter Jones, *The God of Sex* (Colorado Springs, CO: Cook Communications Ministries, 2006), 27. Dr. Jones is the founder is truthXchange, a nonprofit

ministry established to equip Christians to understand and respond to the rising tide of neopaganism. See www.truthXchange.com.

21. *Bob Jones Univ.* at 593, 604; *Norwood v. Harrison* (1973) 413 U.S. 455; *Heart of Atlanta Motel v. United States* (1964) 379 U.S. 241.

22. *Roberts v. United States Jaycees* (1984) 468 U.S. 609; *EEOC v. Fremont Christian School* (9th Cir. 1986) 781 F.2d 1362.

23. *Woodward v. United States* (Fed. Cir. 1989) 871 F.2d 1068, 1076 (primarily behavioral); *Ben-Shalom v. Marsh* (7th Cir. 1989) 881 F.2d 454 (inference of probable conduct); *Richenberg v. Perry* (8th Cir. 1996) 97 F.3d 256 (rebuttable presumption of propensity or intent to engage in conduct); *Thomasson v. Perry* (4th Cir. 1996) 80 F.3d 915 (same); *Philips v. Perry* (9th Cir. 1997) 106 F.3d 1420 (admission of orientation is evidence of conduct); *High Tech Gays v. Defense Industrial Security Clearance Office* (9th Cir. 1990) 895 F.2d 563, 573; *Christian Legal Society v. Walker* (7th Cir. 2006) 453 F.3d 853, 860 (CLS admitted persons with homosexual inclinations but not those who practiced or approved homosexual conduct).

24. *Dale* at 657.

25. *Koebke v. Bernardo Heights Country Club* (2005) 36 Cal.4th 824, 839–840 ("*Koebke*").

26. *Romer v. Evans* (1996) 517 U.S. 620.

27. Stats. 1897, ch. 108, p. 137, § 1, cited in *In re Cox* (1970) 3 Cal.3d 205, 213.

28. *Orloff v. Los Angeles Turf Club* (1951) 36 Cal.2d 734.

29. *Stoumen v. Reilly* (1951) 37 Cal.2d 713.

30. *In re Cox, supra,* 3 Cal.3d at 216.

31. *Marina Point, Ltd. v. Wolfson* (1982) 30 Cal.3d 721.

32. *Hurley v. Irish-American Gay, Lesbian, & Bisexual Group of Boston* (1995) 515 U.S. 557.

33. *Isbister v. Boys Club of Santa Cruz* (1985) 40 Cal.3d 72, 87 (italics added).

34. *Hobbie v. Unemployment Appeals Commission of Florida* (1987) 480 U.S. 136, 142; *Thomas v. Review Bd. of Ind. Employment* (1981) 450 U.S. 707, 708.

35. *Koebke* at 842–843; *Harris v. Capitol Growth Investors, Inc.* (1991) 52 Cal.3d 1142, 1160–61.

36. *Lawrence* at 574, citing *Planned Parenthood of Southeastern Pa. v. Casey* (1992) 505 U.S. 833, 851.

37. 2 Chr. 33:1–11.

38. 2 Chr. 33:12–13.

39. 1 Tim. 1:15.

40. Rom. 3:23.

## Chapter 9

1. *Smith v. FEHC* (1996) 12 Cal.4th 1143 ("*Smith v. FEHC*"); see Red Light Abatement Law, Cal. Penal Code § 11225; *People v. Bhakta* (2006) 37 Cal. Rptr. 3d 652.

2. *North Coast Women's Care Medical Group, Inc. v. Benitez* (2008) 44 Cal.4th 1145 ("*Benitez*").

3. "'Right to 'choose'" not an option for Christian nurse," available at www.alliancedefensefund.org/issues/religiousfreedom/default.aspx?cid=5008&referral=E0709C1C (last visited July 28, 2009).

4. Richard F. Duncan, *Who Wants to Stop the Church: Homosexual Rights Legislation, Public Policy, and Religious Freedom*, 69 Notre Dame L. Rev. 393, 397–398 (1994).

5. Jack S. Vaitayanonta, *In State Legislatures We Trust? The "Compelling Interest" Presumption and Religious Free Exercise Challenges to State Civil Rights Laws*, 101 Colum. L. Rev. 886, 887 (2001).

6. *St. Agnes Hosp. v. Riddick* (D. Md. 1990) 748 F.Supp. 319.

7. *Staver v. Am. Bar Ass'n* (M.D. Fla. 2001) 169 F.Supp.2d 1372; *Zavaletta v. Am. Bar Ass'n* (E.D. Va. 1989) 721 F.Supp. 96.

8. *Bruff v. N. Miss. Health Servs., Inc.* (5th Cir. 2001) 244 F.3d 495.

9. *Lemly v. St. Tammany Parish Hospital* (2009) 8 So.3d 588.

10. *Butler v. Adoption Media, LLC* (N.D. Cal. 2007) 486 F.Supp.2d 1022. See www.alliancedefensefund.org/news/pressrelease.aspx?cid=4128 (last visited July 28, 2009).

11. http://www.ncbar.gov/rules/proprul.asp (last visited on July 21, 2009).

12. Adam Tanner and Mary Milliken, "San Francisco Mayor Condemns Refusal to Marry Gays," *Reuters*, May 22, 2008, available at www.reuters.com/article/domesticNews/idUSN2233433420080523 (last visited on July 21, 2009).

13. *Ocean Grove Camp Meeting Association of the United Methodist Church v. Vespa-Papaleo*, 2007 U.S. Dist. LEXIS 82577.

14. "U.S. Christian Camp Loses Tax-Exempt Status over Same-Sex Civil-Union Ceremony," *Life Site News*, September 19, 2007, available at www.lifesitenews.com/ldn/2007/sep/07091902.html (last visited July 21, 2009).

15. Barbara Bradley Hagerty, "Gay Rights, Religious Liberties: A Three-Act Story," June 16, 2008, available at www.npt.org (last visited July 21, 2009).

16. Chelsea Schilling, "eHarmony.com to match gays," *WorldNetDaily*, November 19, 2008, available at www.wnd.com/index.php?pageId=81446 (last visited July 21, 2009).

17. *United States v. Lee* (1982) 455 U.S. 252, 261 (emphasis added) ("*U.S. v. Lee*").

18. Michael W. McConnell, *"God is Dead and We have Killed Him!" Freedom of Religion in the Post-Modern Age*, 1993 BYU L. Rev. 163, 176.

19. *United States v. Seeger* (1965) 380 U.S. 163, 170.

20. 42 U.S.C. § 300a–7 (2000).

21. 42 U.S.C. § 238n(a)(1) (2000).

22. Douglas Laycock, Ed., *Same-Sex Marriage and Religious Liberty* (Lanham, MD: The Beckett Fund for Religious Liberty and Rowman & Littlefield Publishers, Inc., 2008), Appendix to Chapter 3—Excerpts From Selected State Statutes, pp. 299–310.

23. J. David Bleich, *The Physician as a Conscientious Objector*, 30 Fordham Urb. L. J. 245 (2002).

24. *Chrisman v. Sisters of St. Joseph of Peace* (9th Cir. 1974) 506 F.2d 308 (federal law protects health care workers opposed to sterilization on moral/religious grounds); *Grace Plaza of Great Neck, Inc. v. Elbaum* (App. Div. 1992) 183 A.D.2d 10, 17–19 (patient cannot compel doctor to render treatment contrary to conscience).

25. *Brophy v. New England Sinai Hosp., Inc.* (Mass. 1986) 497 N.E.2d 626 (patient's wife had right to remove him to a facility that would honor his wishes to withhold food and water); *Conservatorship of Morrison* (1988) 206 Cal.App.3d

304, 310 (physician may refuse to withhold life support but must be willing to transfer patient).

26. *In re Requena* (N.J. Super. Ct. Ch. Div. 1986) 517 A.2d 886, 892.

27. *Elbaum v. Grace Plaza of Great Neck, Inc.* (App. Div. 1989) 544 N.Y.S.2d 840, 847.

28. Cal. Const., art. I, § 4.

29. Cal. Const. art. 1, § 8.

30. *State by Cooper v. French* (Minn. 1990) 460 N.W.2d 2, 8–9 ("*State by Cooper*"); *Catholic Charities of Sacramento, Inc. v. Superior Court* (2004) 32 Cal.4th 527, 586 (citing cases in Ohio, Minnesota, and Washington) ("*Catholic Charities*").

31. *Reynolds v. United States* (1878) 98 U.S. 145 (polygamy) ("*Reynolds*"); *Prince v. Massachusetts* (1944) 321 U.S. 158 (child labor) ("*Prince*"); *Jacobson v. Massachusetts* (1905) 197 U.S. 11 (vaccination); *Walker v. Superior Court* (1988) 47 Cal.3d 112 (parental failure to seek medical treatment for child).

32. *Sherbert v. Verner* (1963) 374 U.S. at 403 ("*Sherbert*").

33. See *Smith v. FEHC* at 1174–75; *Catholic Charities* at 565.

34. Nora O'Callaghan, *Lessons From Pharaoh and the Hebrew Midwives: Conscientious Objection to State Mandates as a Free Exercise Right*, 39 Creighton L. Rev. 561, 615–616 (2006).

35. *Church of Lukumi Babalu Aye, Inc. v. City of Hialeah* (1993) 508 U.S. 520, 531 ("*Church of Lukumi Babalu*").

36. Michael W. McConnell, *Religious Freedom at a Crossroads*, 59 U. Chi. L. Rev. 115, 170, 172 (1992).

37. *Valley Hospital Association, Inc. v. Mat-Su Coalition for Choice* (Alaska 1997) 948 P.2d 963.

38. "Senators Clinton and Murray Introduce Legislation to Stop New HHS Rule that Would Undermine Women's Health Care," *United States Senate*, November 20, 2008, available at www.murray.senate.gov/news.cfm?id=305165 (last visited July 22, 2009).

39. "ACLU Files Lawsuit Against Conscience Protection Rules," *Catholic News Agency*, January 17, 2009, available at www.catholicnewsagency.com/new.php?n=14808 (last visited July 22, 2009).

40. *United States v. Kozminski* (1988) 487 U.S. 931, 942–943.

41. *Poultry Producers v. Barlow* (1922) 189 Cal. 278, 288.

42. *Stoumen v. Reilly*, (1951) 37 Cal.2d 713 (restaurant service); *Rolon v. Kulwitzky* (1984) 153 Cal.App.3d 289 (restaurant seating); *Koebke v. Bernardo Heights Country Club* (2005) 36 Cal.4th 824 (country club rights).

43. *Leach v. Drummond Medical Group, Inc.* (1983) 144 Cal.App.3d 362.

44. *Frisby v. Schultz* (1988) 487 U.S. 474, 485.

45. Richard F. Duncan, *Who Wants to Stop the Church* at 396.

46. Marc L. Rubinstein, *Note, Gay Rights and Religion: A Doctrinal Approach to the Argument that Anti-Gay-Rights Initiatives Violate the Establishment Clause*, 46 Hastings L.J. 1585, 1613 (1995).

47. *Wooley v. Maynard* (1977) 430 U.S. 705, 714; *West Virginia State Bd. of Educ. v. Barnette* (1943) 319 U.S. 624.

48. *Hurley v. Irish-American Gay, Lesbian, & Bisexual Group of Boston* (1995) 515 U.S. 557, 575.

49. *Boy Scouts of Am. v. Dale* (2000) 530 U.S. 640, 654.

50. *Ibid.* at 698.

51. *Benitez*.

52. Courtney Miller, *Note, Reflections on Protecting Conscience for Health Care Providers: A Call for More Inclusive Statutory Protection in Light of Constitutional Considerations*, 15 S. Cal. Rev. L. & Social Justice 327, 340–341, 344 (2006).

53. Nora O'Callaghan, *Lessons From Pharaoh* at 573.

54. Michael W. McConnell, *"God is Dead and We have Killed Him!"* at 186–188.

55. Harlan Loeb and David Rosenberg, *Fundamental Rights in Conflict: The Price of a Maturing Democracy*, 77 N.D. L. Rev. 27, 42 (2001).

56. Alvin C. Lin, NOTE: *Sexual Orientation Antidiscrimination Laws and the Religious Liberty Protection Act: The Pitfalls of the Compelling State Interest Inquiry*, 89 Geo. L.J. 719, 734 (2001).

57. *Board of Directors of Rotary International v. Rotary Club of Duarte* (1987) 481 U.S. 537, 549; *Roberts v. United States Jaycees* (1984) 468 U.S. 609, 628.

58. *Gonzales v. O Centro Espirita Beneficente* (2006) 126 S. Ct. 1211, 1220, 1223–24 ("*O Centro*").

59. *Wisconsin v. Yoder* (1972) 406 U.S. 205, 221, 236 ("*Yoder*").

60. *U.S. v. Lee* at 259.

61. *Romer v. Evans* (1996) 517 U.S. 620.

62. *Equality Foundation of Greater Cincinnati v. City of Cincinnati* (6th Cir. 1997) 128 F.3d 289, 294, 300.

63. *Gay Rights Coalition of Georgetown Univ. Law Ctr. v. Georgetown Univ.* (D.C. 1987) 536 A.2d 1, 32 ("*Gay Rights Coalition*"); *Benitez*.

64. *Gay Rights Coalition* at 32.

65. *Kerrigan v. Commissioner of Public Health* (2008) 289 Conn. 135.

66. *Varnum v. Brien* (2009) 763 N.W.2d 862.

67. *In re Marriage Cases* (2008) 43 Cal. 4th 757.

68. *Goodridge v. Dept. of Public Health* (2003) 440 Mass. 309.

69. *Thomas v. Review Bd. of Ind. Employment Sec. Div.* (1981) 450 U.S. 707 ("*Thomas v. Review Bd.*").

70. *Rasmussen v. Glass* (Minn. Ct. App. 1993) 498 N.W.2d 508, 510–511.

71. *Blanding v. Sports & Health Club, Inc.* (Minn. Ct. App. 1985) 373 N.W.2d 784, 791.

72. Jennifer Tetenbaum Miller, *Note, Free Exercise v. Legal Ethics: Can a Religious Lawyer Discriminate in Choosing Clients?*, 13 Geo. J. Legal Ethics 161, 166–167, 182 (1999).

73. *Sherbert*; *Thomas v. Review Bd.*; *Hobbie v. Unemployment Appeals Commission of Florida* (1987) 480 U.S. 136 ("*Hobbie*"); *Frazee v. Ill. Dept. of Employment Sec.* (1989) 489 U.S. 829.

74. *Bob Jones Univ. v. United States* (1983) 461 U.S. 574 ("*Bob Jones Univ.*").

75. *Bowen v. Roy* (1986) 476 U.S. 693 ("*Bowen v. Roy*").

76. *Valov v. DMV, supra*, 132 Cal.App.4th 1113.

77. *CLS v. Walker* (7th Cir. 2006) 453 F.3d 853.

78. *Bowen v. Roy* at 704.

79. *Ibid.* at 703.

80. *Sherbert* at 412; *Thomas v. Review Bd.* at 716; *Hobbie* at 141.

81. Alvin C. Lin, *Note, Sexual Orientation Antidiscrimination Laws and the Religious Liberty Protection Act* at 731–732.

82. *Braunfeld v. Brown* (1961) 366 U.S. 599, 605–606.

83. *Bob Jones Univ.*

84. *Tony and Susan Alamo Foundation v. Secretary of Labor* (1985) 471 U.S. 290.

85. *U.S. v. Lee.*

86. *Gay Rights Coalition.*

87. *EEOC v. Fremont Christian School* (9th Cir. 1986) 781 F.2d 1362; *Catholic Charities.*

88. *Reynolds.*

89. *Prince* (child labor laws).

90. *Yoder.*

91. *Div., Ore. Dept. of Human Res. v. Smith* (1990) 494 U.S. 872; *O Centro.*

92. *Yoder* at 218; *Bowen v. Roy* at 704.

93. Richard F. Duncan, *Who Wants to Stop the Church* at 414; Nora O'Callaghan, *Lessons From Pharaoh* at 562.

94. *Smith v. FEHC* at 1170; *Swanner v. Anchorage Equal Rights Commission* (Alaska 1994) 874 P.2d 274; *State by Cooper, McCready v. Hoffius I* (Mich. 1998) 586 N.W.2d 723, vacated and remanded at *McCready v. Hoffius II* (Mich. 1999) 593 N.W.2d 545.

95. Jennifer Tetenbaum Miller, NOTE: *Free Exercise v. Legal Ethics: Can a Religious Lawyer Discriminate in Choosing Clients?*, 13 Geo. J. Legal Ethics 161, 170, 177 (1999).

96. *Yoder* at 218.

97. Nora O'Callaghan, *Lessons From Pharaoh* at 612–613.

98. Michael W. McConnell, *The Origins and Historical Understanding of Free Exercise of Religion*, 103 Harv. L. Rev. 1409, 1420 (1990) (discussing definitions of "neutrality").

99. Richard F. Duncan, *Who Wants to Stop the Church* at 422, n113; *Church of Lukumi Babalu* at 562 (Souter, J., concurring); Douglas Laycock, *Formal, Substantive, and Disaggregated Neutrality Toward Religion*, 39 DePaul L. Rev. 993, 1001 (1990).

100. Marc L. Rubinstein, *Note, Gay Rights and Religion* at 1612.

101. Teresa S. Collett, *Heads, Secularists Win; Tails, Believers Lose—Returning Only Free Exercise to the Political Process*, 20 U. Ark. Little Rock L.J. 689, 697 (1998).

## Chapter 10

1. This victory occurred through the efforts of Alliance Defense Fund. The story is available at www.alliancedefensefund.org/news/pressrelease.aspx?cid=4098 (last visited July 24, 2009).

2. This is another successful Alliance Defense Fund case. A more detailed account is available at www.alliancedefensefund.org/news/pressrelease. aspx?cid=4090 (last visited July 24, 2009).

3. *McGowan v. Maryland* (1961) 366 U.S. 420.

4. *Braunfeld v. Brown* (1961) 366 U.S. 599.

5. *Thornton v. Caldor* (1985) 472 U.S. 703.

6. *Marsh v. Chambers* (1983) 463 U.S. 783.

7. www.telladf.org/prayerpolicies. For further information and links, see www. alliancedefensefund.org/news/story.aspx?cid=4195 (last visited July 24, 2009).

Alliance Defense Fund's website contains numerous press releases about specific cases where they have provided assistance to local governments.

8. Recently, Forsyth County, North Carolina lost a battle in federal district court concerning sectarian prayers to opening meetings of the County Commissioners. The Commissioners are appealing this decision to the Fourth Circuit Court of Appeals.

9. *Lynch v. Donnelly* (1984) 465 U.S. 668.

10. *County of Allegheny v. American Civil Liberties Union, Greater Pittsburgh Chapter* (1989) 492 U.S. 573.

11. *Capital Square Review and Advisory Bd. v. Pinette* (1995) 515 U.S. 753.

12. See www.alliancedefensefund.org/news/pressrelease.aspx?cid=2624 and www.saychristmas.org (for more information about the Christmas Project and many more examples of unlawful censorship) (last visited July 25, 2009). See also Alan Sears and Craig Osten, *The ACLU vs. America*, Chapter 7, "The ACLU vs. Christmas" (Nashville, TN: Broadman & Holman Publishers, 2005).

13. Alan Sears, "It's OK to Say Merry Christmas," November 24, 2004, available at www.alliancedefensefund.org/news/story.aspx?cid=3229 (last visited July 25, 2009).

14. *Pleasant Grove City v. Summum* (2009) 129 S.Ct. 1125. The city was represented by attorney Jay Sekulow with the American Center for Law & Justice (ACLJ).

15. *Modrovich v. Allegheny County*, 385 F.3d 397, 410–11 (3d Cir. 2004).

16. *Van Orden v. Perry*, 545 U.S. 677, 681 (2005).

17. *Ibid.* at 690–692; *see also ACLU Neb. Found. v. City of Plattsmouth*, 419 F.3d 772 (8th Cir. 2005).

18. *O'Connor v. Washburn Univ.*, 416 F.3d 1216 (10th Cir. 2004).

19. *Stone v. Graham* (1980) 449 U.S. 39, 42.

20. *McCreary County v. ACLU* (2005) 545 U.S. 844.

21. "Ten Commandments Judge Removed From Office," November 14, 2003, available at www.cnn.com/2003/LAW/11/13/moore.tencommandments/ (last visited August 22, 2009).

22. *Glassroth v. Moore* (M.D. Ala. 2002) 242 F. Supp. 2d 1068.

23. *Glassroth v. Moore* (M.D. Ala. 2002) 229 F. Supp. 2d 1290.

24. Information about the Foundation for Moral Law is available at www.morallaw.org.

25. *Buono v. Norton* (C.D. Cal. 2002) 212 F. Supp. 2d 1202, 1204–1205, 1215–1217.

26. *Buono v. Kempthorne*, 527 F.3d 758 (9th Cir. 2008).

27. *Salazar v. Buono*, USSC Docket No. 08–472 (oral argument in the U.S. Supreme Court is scheduled for October 7, 2009).

28. *Newdow v. Cong. of the United States* (E.D. Cal. 2006) 435 F. Supp. 2d 1066.

29. *Elk Grove Unified Sch. Dist. v. Newdow*, 542 U.S. 1 (2004).

30. *Ibid.* at 44–45.

## Chapter II

1. "Ten-year-old student and friends told to put away their Bibles during recess," May 11, 2005, available at www.alliancedefensefund.org/main/general/print.aspx?cid=3420 (last visited August 22, 2009).

2. "Backed by ADF, first-grade student now permitted to share Christmas song with classmates," December 15, 2006, available at www.alliancedefensefund.org/news/pressrelease.aspx?cid=3953 (last visited August 22, 2009).

3. *O.T. v. Frenchtown Elem. Sch. Dist. Bd. of Educ.* (D.N.J. 2006) 465 F. Supp. 2d 369.

4. "Schoolteachers allowed to exercise their right to participate in 'See You at the Pole,'" September 28, 2006, available at www.alliancedefensefund.org/news/pressrelease.aspx?cid=3866 (last visited August 22, 2009).

5. "School's stealth attempt to show sexually explicit film thwarted by ADF," June 27, 2006, available at www.alliancedefensefund.org/news/pressrelease.aspx?cid=3788 (last visited August 22, 2009).

6. *Engel v. Vitale* (1962) 370 U.S. 421.

7. *Ibid.* at 422.

8. *Ibid.* at 425.

9. *Ibid.* at 423.

10. *Ibid.* at 424.

11. *Ibid.* at 449 (Stewart, J., dissenting).

12. *Wallace v. Jaffree* (1985) 472 U.S. 38.

13. *Lee v. Weisman* (1992) 505 U.S. 577.

14. *Santa Fe. Indep. Sch. Dist. v. Doe* (2000) 530 U.S. 290.

15. *Minersville School District v. Gobitis* (1940) 310 U.S. 586.

16. *West Virginia State Board of Education v. Barnette* (1943) 319 U.S. 624.

17. This information is widely available online, including www.free2pray.info.

18. Stephen D. Solomon, *Ellery's Protest: How One Young Man Defied Tradition and Sparked the Battle over School Prayer* (Ann Arbor: The University of Michigan Press, 2007), 1–4. This book gives a detailed history of Ellery Schempp's journey to the Supreme Court.

19. *Abington Township School District v. Schempp* (1963) 374 U.S. 203.

20. *Murray v. Curlett* (1962) 228 Md. 239.

21. *Stone v. Graham* (1980) 449 U.S. 39.

22. Rom. 6:2, 15.

23. *Cochran v. Louisiana Board of Education* (1930) 281 U.S. 370.

24. *Board of Education v. Allen* (1968) 392 U.S. 236.

25. *Committee for Public Education and Religious Liberty v. Nyquist* (1973) 413 U.S. 756.

26. *Meek v. Pittenger* (1975) 421 U.S. 349, partially overruled in *Mitchell v. Helms* (2000) 530 U.S. 793, another case about providing materials and equipment to private schools.

27. *Wolman v. Walter* (1977) 433 U.S. 229, partially overruled in *Mitchell v. Helms* (2000) 530 U.S. 793.

28. *Committee for Public Education and Religious Liberty v. Regan* (1980) 444 U.S. 646.

29. *Mueller v. Allen* (1983) 463 U.S. 388.

30. *Aguilar v. Felton* (1985) 473 U.S. 402.

31. *Grand Rapids School v. Ball* (1985) 473 U.S. 373.

32. *Zobrest v. Catalina Foothills School District* (1993) 509 U.S. 1.

33. *Agostini v. Felton* (1997) 521 U.S. 203.

34. *Mitchell v. Helms* (2000) 530 U.S. 793, partially overruling *Meek v. Pittenger* (1975) 421 U.S. 349 and *Wolman v. Walter* (1977) 433 U.S. 229.

35. *Zelman v. Simmons-Harris* (2002) 536 U.S. 639.

36. *Tilton v. Richardson* (1971) 403 U.S. 672.

37. *Roemer v. Board of Public Works* (1976) 426 U.S. 736.

38. *Pierce v. Society of Sisters* (1925) 268 U.S. 510, 534–535.

39. *Wisconsin v. Yoder* (1972) 406 U.S. 205.

40. *Troxel v. Granville* (2000) 530 U.S. 57.

41. *Prince v. Massachusetts* (1944) 321 U.S. 158.

42. *Ibid.* at 167.

43. *Parker v. Hurley* (1st Cir. 2008) 514 F.3d 87.

44. *California Education Committee v. Jack O'Connell*, Superior Court of the State of California, County of San Diego, Case No. 37–2008–00077546 -CU-CRCTL. For further information and updates, see www.faith-freedom.com/in-the-courts.

45. Cal. Educ. Code § 210.7, enacted by Senate Bill 777, effective January 1, 2008.

46. "Education Secretary Announces Nine Senior Staff Appointments," U.S. Department of Education press release, May 19, 2009, available at www.ed.gov/news/pressreleases/2009/05/05192009d.html (last visited July 28, 2009).

47. *Scopes v. State* (1927) 154 Tenn. 105.

48. *Epperson v. Arkansas* (1968) 393 U.S. 97.

49. *Edwards v. Aguillard* (1987) 482 U.S. 578.

## Chapter 12

1. *Loya v. County of Orange, et. al.*, Orange County Superior Court, State of California, Case No. 30–2009–00118619, filed on February 13, 2009.

2. *EEOC v. Townley Engineering* (9th Cir. 1988) 859 F.2d 610, 624–625 (Noonan, J., dissenting).

3. 42 U.S.C. §§ 2000 *et seq.*

4. *Trans World Airlines v. Hardison* (1977) 432 U.S. 63.

5. *Endres v. Ind. State Police* (7th Cir. 2003) 349 F.3d 922.

6. *Lotosky v. Univ. of Rochester* (W.D.N.Y. 2002) 192 F.Supp.2d 127.

7. *Hellinger v. Eckerd Corp.* (S.D. Fla. 1999) 67 F.Supp.2d 1359.

8. *Brady v. Dean* (Vt. 2001) 790 A.2d 428, 435.

9. *Bruff v. N. Miss. Health Servs., Inc.* (5th Cir. 2001) 244 F.3d 495.

10. *Garcetti v. Ceballos* (2006) 547 U.S. 410.

11. *Tucker v. Cal. Dept. of Education* (9th Cir. 1996) 97 F.3d 1204.

12. *Altman v. Minn. Dept. of Corrections* (8th Cir. 2001) 251 F.3d 1199.

13. *Good News Employee Assn. v. Hicks* (9th Cir. 1007) 223 Fed. Appx. 734.

14. *Peterson v. Hewlett Packard Co.* (9th Cir. 2004) 358 F.3d 599, 602.

15. *Moranski v. Gen. Motors Corp.* (S.D. Ind. 2005) 2005 WL 552419, *aff'd,* 433 F.3d 537 (7th Cir. 2005).

16. *Buonanno v. AT&T Broadband, LLC* (D. Colo. 2004) 313 F.Supp.2d 1069, 1074–75.

17. *Ibid.*, at 1075–76 (emphasis added).

18. *EEOC v. Townley Engineering* (9th Cir. 1988) 859 F.2d 610.

19. *State ex rel. McClure v. Sports & Health Club, Inc.* (Minn. 1985) 370 N.W.2d 844.

20. *Erdmann v. Tranquility, Inc.* (N.D. Cal. 2001) 155 F.Supp.2d 1152.

21. *Fairchild v. Riva Jewelry Mfg.* (N.Y. Sup. Ct. 2007) 2007 N.Y. Misc. Lexis 4912.

22. *Ibid.*

24. *McConnell v. Anderson* (8th Cir. 1971) 451 F.2d 193, 198.

24. *Chambers v. Omaha Girls Club* (8th Cir. 1987) 834 F.2d 697.

## Chapter 13

1. *Walker v. First Presbyterian Church* (Cal. Super. Ct. 1980) 22 Fair Empl. Prac. Cas. (BNA) 762.

2. *Baker v. Nachtrieb* (1856) 60 U.S. 126.

3. *Order of St. Benedict v. Steinhauser* (1914) 234 U.S. 640.

4. *Watson v. Jones* (1872) 80 U.S. 679.

5. *PCUSA v. Mary Elizabeth Blue Hull Memorial Presbyterian Church* (1969) 393 U.S. 440.

6. *Kedroff v. St. Nicholas Cathedral* (1952) 344 U.S. 94.

7. *Serbian Eastern Orthodox Diocese for the U.S.A. and Canada v. Milivojevich* (1976) 426 U.S. 696.

8. *Doe v. Lutheran High School* (2005) 702 N.W.2d 322.

9. *Walker v. First Presbyterian Church* (Cal. Super. Ct. 1980) 22 Fair Empl. Prac. Cas. (BNA) 762.

10. *Gunn v. Mariners Church* (Cal. App. 2008) 167 Cal.App.4th 206.

11. *Boyd v. Harding Acad., Inc.* (6th Cir. 1996) 88 F.3d 410.

12. *Cline v. Catholic Diocese* (6th Cir. 2000) 206 F.3d 651, 658.

13. *Ganzy v. Allen Christian Sch.* (E.D.N.Y. 1998) 995 F.Supp. 340.

14. *Hall v. Baptist Memorial Health Care Corp.* (6th Cir. 2000) 215 F.3d 618.

15. *Madsen v. Erwin* (Mass. 1985) 481 N.E.2d 1160.

16. "Court Suggests Church Split; Case Heads to Ninth Circuit," July 21, 2009. See www.pacificjustice.org/news/court-suggests-church-split-case-heads-ninth-circuit (last visited August 5, 2009).

17. 42 U.S.C. § 2000cc et seq.

18. 42 U.S.C. § 2000cc(a)(1).

19. *Dausch v. Rykse* (7th Cir. 1994) 52 F.3d 1425; *Sanders v. Casa View Baptist Church* (5th Cir. 1998) 134 F.3d 331. This is a recurring theme in church counseling cases.

20. *Westbrook v. Penley* (2007) 231 S.W.3d 389, 391–392.

21. *People v. Hodges* (1992) 10 Cal. App. 4th Supp. 20.

22. *Tarasoff v. Regents of University of California* (1976) 17 Cal. 3d 425.

23. *Nally v. Grace Community Church* (1988) 47 Cal. 3d 278.

24. *Jacqueline R. v. Household of Faith Family Church, Inc.* (2002) 97 Cal. App.4th 198.

25. *Odenthal v. Seventh-Day Adventists* (Minn. 2002) 649 N.W.2d 426.

26. *Wende C. and David C. v. United Methodist Church* (2004) 776 N.Y.S.2d 390.

27. *Richelle L. v. Roman Catholic Archbishop* (2003) 106 Cal. App. 4th 257.

28. *Hester v. Barnett* (Mo. App. 1987) 723 S.W.2d 544.

29. *Guinn v. The Church of Christ of Collinsville* (1989) 775 P.2d 766.

30. *Smith v. Calvary Christian Church* (Mich. 2000) 614 N.W.2d 590.

31. Peacemaker Ministries is a wonderful resource for materials and training to help churches prevent litigation: www.peacemaker.net.

# Chapter 14

1. *Harper v. Poway Unified Sch. Dist.* (S.D. Cal. 2004) 345 F.Supp.2d 1096, aff'd, (9th Cir. 2006) 445 F.3d 1166.

2. *Harper v. Poway Unified Sch. Dist.* (2007) 549 U.S. 1262.

3. http://www.huffingtonpost.com/2009/05/31/george-tiller-killed-abor_n_209504.html.

4. *Planned Parenthood of Southeastern Pennsylvania v. Casey* (1992) 505 U.S. 833, 866.

5. *FEC v. Mass. Citizens for Life* (1986) 479 U.S. 238.

6. *Frisby v. Schultz* (1988) 487 U.S. 474.

7. *Bray (Operation Rescue) v. Alexandria Women's Health Clinic* (1993) 506 U.S. 263.

8. *Madsen v. Women's Health Center* (1994) 512 U.S. 753.

9. *Schenck v. Pro-Choice Network* (1997) 519 U.S. 357.

10. 20 U.S.C.S. §§ 4071–4074.

11. *Good News Club v. Milford Cent. Sch.* (2001) 533 U.S. 98.

12. *Widmar v. Vincent* (1981) 454 U.S. 263.

13. *Lamb's Chapel v. Center Moriches Union Free School District* (1993) 508 U.S. 384.

14. *Rosenberger v. University of Virginia* (1995) 515 U.S. 819.

15. *Tinker v. Des Moines Indep. Cmty. Sch. Dist.* (1969) 393 U.S. 503.

16. *Bethel Sch. Dist. No. 403 v. Fraser* (1986) 478 U.S. 675. See also *Caudillo v. Lubbock Independent School District* (N.D. Texas 2004) 311 F.Supp.2d 550, where the court upheld a school's refusal to allow a homosexual student group to meet on campus because the club's website had links to legally obscene material.

17. *Hazelwood Sch. Dist. v. Kuhlmeier* (1988) 484 U.S. 260.

18. *Morse v. Frederick* (2007) 551 U.S. 393.

19. *Nixon v. N. Local Sch. Dist. Bd. of Ed. (S.D. Ohio 2005)* 383 F.Supp.2d 965.

20. *Hansen v. Ann Arbor Sch.* (E.D. Mich. 2003) 293 F.Supp.2d 780, 782–783.

21. *Citizens for a Responsible Curriculum v. Montgomery County Pub. Sch.* (D. Md. 2005) 2005 WL 1075634, 2005 U.S. Dist. LEXIS 8130.

22. *Busch v. Marple Newton School District* (3d. Cir. 2009) 567 F.3d 89.

23. *Slee v. Commissioner* (2nd Cir. 1930) 42 F.2d 184; cited in *Christian Echoes National Ministry, Inc. v. U.S.* (10th Cir. 1972) 470 F.2d 849, 854.

24. *Branch Ministries v. Internal Revenue Service*, 211 F.3d 137, 140 (2000) (emphasis added).

25. "Swedish pastor who spoke about homosexuality from pulpit cleared of "hate crime" conviction," February 14, 2005, available online at www.alliancedefensefund.org/news/pressrelease.aspx?cid=3335 (last visited August 8, 2009).

26. *Hellquist v. Owens*, 2002 Sask. Q.B. 506, rev'd, 2006 Sask. Ct. App. 41.

27. www.nationformarriage.org.

28. *Okwedy v. Molinari* (2d Cir. 2003) 333 F.3d 339.

29. *Canyon Ferry Baptist Church v. Unsworth* (9th Cir. 2009) 556 F.3d 1021.

30. H.R. 3302, 109th Cong., 1st Sess., July 14, 2005.

31. Jay Sekulow, "More Calls to Reinstate 'Fairness Doctrine,'" February 16, 2009, available at www.aclj.org/TrialNotebook/Read.aspx?id=735 (last visited August 7, 2009).

32. H.R. 226.

33. *Peterson v. Hewlett Packard Co.* (9th Cir. 2004) 358 F.3d 599, 604 (emphasis added).

## Chapter 15

1. Arthur Delaney, "Obama: U.S. Not a Christian Nation or a Jewish Nation or a Muslim Nation," April 6, 2009, The Huffington Post, available online at www.huffingtonpost.com/2009/04/06/obama-us-not-a-christian_n_183772.html (last visited August 10, 2009).

2. "National and State Leaders Seek to Honor Harvey Milk," August 7, 2009, available online at www.faith-freedom.com/news (last visited August 11, 2009).

3. "In California, a Federal Court Backhands Another Assault on Marriage," July 28, 2009, available online at www.alliancedefensefund.org/issues/traditional-family/samesexmarriage.aspx?cid=5019&referral=E0809B1L (last visited August 11, 2009).

4. *Perry v. Schwarzenegger.* See news and updates from Alliance Defense Fund at http://www.alliancedefensefund.org/news/pressrelease.aspx?cid=5162 (last visited March 3, 2010).

5. "Modesto School Board May Let Students Get Abortions Without Parents' Knowledge," July 28, 2009, available online at www.pacificjustice.org/news/modesto-school-board-may-let-students-get-abortions-without-parents-knowledge (last visited August 11, 2009).